SO YOU WANT TO DATE MY DAUGHTER?

A Father's Rulebook on the Do's and Don'ts for Dating His Little Princess

COREY LEE WILSON

So You Want to Date My Daughter?

A Father's Rulebook on the Do's and Don'ts for Dating His Little Princess

Copyright © 2018 by Corey Lee Wilson

All rights reserved. No part of this book may be reproduced in any manner without the express written consent of the publisher, except in the case of brief excerpts in all types of written media. All inquiries for such can be made below.

Fratire Publishing books can be purchased in bulk with special discounts for educational purposes, association gifts, sales promotions, and special editions can be created to specifications. All inquiries for such can be made below.

FRATIRE PUBLISHING LLC
P.O. Box 78148
1941 California Ave.
Corona, CA 92877
FratirePublishing@att.net
(951) 638-5502

Visit our websites at www.FratirePublishing.com for more titles by Corey Lee Wilson and www.SYWTDMD.net for more information about this book or e-mail us as well at FratirePublishing@att.net.

Printed in the United States of America

First Edition: (February) 2018
10 9 8 7 6 5 4 3 2 1

ISBN 978-0-9847490-1-0

Cover design by Ever Juarez

So You Want to Date My Daughter?

A Father's Rulebook on the Do's and Don'ts for Dating His Little Princess

This book is dedicated to my daughter Katrina Isabella Wilson and every other daughter and dad (and moms too) with a teenage daughter out there that can benefit from one like this.

Thanks Ever Juarez for the great cover design and graphics, both Adam D. Denbo and Liz Perez for proofreading, and Dave von Fleckles for teaching me how to become a gentleman.

I would also like to thank the Brothers of the Delta Tau Chapter of the Phi Kappa Tau Fraternity for providing the location, the actors, video and graphic production, as well as support for the making of the "So You Want to Date My Daughter?" video.

So You Want to Date My Daughter?

A Father's Rulebook on the Do's and Don'ts for Dating His Little Princess

Table of Contents

Table of Contents vi
Foreword – Welcome to Fratire Publishing 1
Preface – Why I Wrote This Book 3
1 – How Young is Too Young to Start Dating? 5
2 – Preparing Your Daughter for Dating 18
3 – Best Dates and Practices for Your Daughter 30
4 – Sound Dating Advice for the Candidate 43
5 – Setting Boundaries and Establishing the Rules of Engagement . 55
6 – Meeting the Parents and the Candidate Interview 68
7 – A Single Parent's Playbook 79
8 – Parenting Styles and Dating Forms 90
9 – The Art of Dating 106
10 – 100 Dating Ideas 120
11 – The 411 on Online Dating 128
12 – Chaperoning, Proms, Parties and Driving 137
13 – A Sex Education Primer 150
14 – Adolescence Development and Behavior 159
15 – Risky Behavior and Teenage Pregnancy 170
16 – Sexually Transmitted Diseases and Infections 181
17 – Teen Dating Violence and Unhealthy Relationships 196
18 – Worst Possible Candidates 207
19 – Least Desirable Candidates 209
20 – Best Possible Candidates 211
21 – The End of Innocence 213
Closing 224
Afterword 226

Appendix 228
Glossary – Dating Slang and Teenage Jargon 229
Resources 232
Index 243
Biography 249

Foreword – Welcome to Fratire Publishing

So, what is "fratire" you ask?

Fratire is a combination of the words "fraternity" and "satire" and represents a new genre of literature that uses in your face satire to make a point and at the same time do it from a tough love approach that respects the fraternal kinship of human nature. It's also about common sense books for common sense people and places more emphasis on the practical side of changing human behavior for the better, even if our feelings get hurt a little along the way.

Fratire Publishing format and content style is a mastery of presentation and organization, ease of use straight forward facts and quick summaries. Strategically, we use a lot of statistics to make a point or show a comparison from a global perspective. However, we also recognize that every person must be treated with equal opportunity and fairness, free of bias and prejudices, and seen as a unique individual, like no other.

Our approach is about relevant books for sapient beings covering a range of useful and timely topics and practical knowledge. As a self-publisher and Founder and President of Fratire Publishing, my mission and goal in life to provide common sense books and how-to guides to help everyday people navigate safely through the many hazards of life, be it dating, character building, or philosophical perspectives.

Our vision of Sapience is becoming a person of/or showing great wisdom and sound judgment, and our mission is taking action to advance society with personal intelligence and enlightenment as well as working now and together with others; to make the world a better place. If this sounds like you and you can never have enough common sense, wisdom and relevancy, then come and visit us and learn more at www.FratirePublishing.com.

That's why I wrote this non-fiction book titled ***So You Want to Date My Daughter? A Father's Rulebook on the Do's and Don'ts of Dating His Little Princess***. However, more needs to be done regarding gentlemanly and ladylike dating behavior, so I saw the need to write two companion books, ***Every Daughter Deserves a Gentleman*** and ***Every Son Deserves a Lady*** as well. On top of that, Fratire Publishing is donating ten-percent of these book's sales to the Times Up Now organization to help prevent sexual harassment and misogyny.

Want to be part of the solution to help end the problem of sexual harassment and misogynistic behavior? If the answer is yes, here is how you can help by igniting a national petition for a presidential proclamation to make every April the **"Be a Gentleman" and "Be a Lady" Month**. Ultimately, the goal of course is to practice gentlemanly and ladylike qualities every month, week and day of the year 365/24/7.

To learn more about becoming a sponsor, please visit our website at: www.GentlemanandLady.com. For more information about developing and promoting gentlemanly and ladylike behaviors, please follow these links to the **Every Daughter Deserves A Gentleman Program** at www.EDDAG.net and/or the **Every Son Deserves A Lady Program** at www.ESDAL.net and complete a short contact form to be added to our subscriber list.

Preface – Why I Wrote This Book

It finally hit me one day after I kept hearing my tween aged daughter rave time and time again after she saw a good-looking guy. "Boy! Is he hot?" "He's so hot!" "He's smokin' hot!" So, it got me thinking; 'Maybe she's going to end up wild and promiscuous like my single Playboy Bunny mom!' Worried like any loving father, I remembered articles on how family traits skip a generation. If that were true for my daughter, she could end up being a *Playboy* centerfold ten years later!

Determined to make sure that didn't happen, I did extensive research regarding teenage dating and sexuality while she was a teenager, covering every pertinent fact and statistic regarding teenage dating and sexuality. What I discovered during this journey of enlightenment there was NO definitive book about teenage sexuality and dating! I decided to become an expert myself on the comical, emotional, and humiliating aspects of adolescent behavior, as well as the darker side of teenage pregnancy, STDs, and intimate partner violence.

Knowing what I wanted then as a testosterone fueled teenage boy versus what I know now as a protective father of teenage daughter, I sat down and wrote **So You Want to Date My Daughter? A Father's Rulebook on the Do's and Don'ts for Dating His Little Princess**, the definitive book for every-day-dads and parents like you and me who need a how-to-manual in life. Because of that and what I learned along the way, it's now this book's mission to help prepare and empower other dads and daughters (and moms too) for safe and sane dating and pass this practical information along from every chapter.

So how did my daughter make it through her teenage dating years you might ask? Did she turn out to be wild and promiscuous like her Playboy Bunny grandmother? I'm relieved to inform you, we both made it safely through her teenage dating years, without any incidences, and she's a mature and responsible adult now, and turned out better than any dad could hope for. Yours can too with some straight forward advice, practical knowledge and preparation.

Yours truly,

Corey Lee Wilson
Author & Publisher

1 – How Young is Too Young to Start Dating?

This may be the first question most parents ask themselves about their teenage daughter dating: How young is too young to start dating?

A good question with no definitive answer. The truth is there is no right age. You need to know your child's stage of development and maturity level along with your family values. And just like the saying "one size does not fit all" the same concept applies to how young is too young for your daughter to start dating.

There certainly isn't an automatic age when tweens (ages 10 to 12) and teens (ages 13 to 18) are ready to date. The age range for starting to date can vary from a casual tween group date at age ten to a romantic dinner for two teenagers at age nineteen. As a parent, you should try to avoid making a rule that says, "No dating until you're sixteen," or something along those lines.

If you're not quite sure what the terms tween, preteen, teen, teenager and adolescent mean, no problem, here are some quick definitions before we get started.

> ➤ A **tween**, or **preteen**, is usually between the ages of ten and twelve years old, in the fifth to seventh grades. The tween stage typically ends with the onset of puberty and/or age thirteen.

- A **teen**, or **teenager**, is a young person whose age falls within an age range of 13 - 18 and their age number ends in "teen" as in thirteen years old. They've typically started puberty and are maturing into adulthood. Teens aged from 19 - 21 are considered young adults.

- **Adolescence** is the name for the transition period from childhood to adulthood. Both tweens and teens are **adolescents**. The highpoint of adolescence is during puberty, a period of rapid mental and physical development.

My Daughter is Too Young to Date!

I know there are many fathers out there who are thinking they might be able to put off the dating process for a little while. Maybe indefinitely! But let's get real because most dads and daughters are not prepared when a teenage boy or young man comes-a-calling for your daughter, you'll be unprepared for it and have missed a great opportunity to help mold and guide your daughter's dating experience for the better.

The best way to manage this process is to start early and have a plan. That's what this guidebook gives you; a plan of action for safe and sane dating and some great ideas and strategies to carry it through.

From here on, the term **candidate** is what a daughter's date is referred to in this book and refers to a boy in any stage development; be it a tween, teen, or young adult. The freshly coined term **candidon't** is used to designate an unworthy candidate.

When the time comes to talk to your children about relationships, sex, and intimacy, it's never too early. Parents should have as many teachable moments and as many opportunities to discuss dating as possible. There are some things in parenthood where the father has more of a positive (and negative) impact on their children's lives, and dating is one of them. How well a father handles this process and establishes safe and sane dating rules and practices can ultimately determine if your daughter ends up with an acceptable candidate or an unacceptable candidate, or a "candidon't" as used in this book.

However, rules without a positive relationship between parent and teenager can lead to rebellion. If your daughter doesn't agree with all of your dating rules, she'll at least know that you're interested in whom she dates and if they're good enough for her. And when she understands that you're looking out for her best interest, she'll come to love and respect you even more for it. Well, that's the idea!

Is Your Daughter Ready to Date?

Most tweens and teens interviewed say they're frustrated and upset because their mom, dad or both, say they're too young to date. What most kids don't realize though is that parents set these kinds of rules for them because they love their kids and they want the best for them.

Most parents feel plenty of anxiety when they think about their kids growing up and starting to date. They worry about them growing up too fast or engaging in sexual activity before they're ready, and they also fear that dating might distract their children from homework and after-school activities.

Tween Dating

Tweens are "in-between" being a child and a teen. They are children in the sense that they are not yet teenagers, but they differ from small children in that they are not primarily occupied with play. They're often going through a period of rapid social, physiological and emotional development known as puberty. The tween years are a time of the most rapid and dramatic change in development since conception.

Parents continue to believe "not my child" when it comes to sexual relationships with their tweens and teens. As it turns out, they're much more sexually advanced than we give them credit for and that's cause for concern! Of the parents who say that sex is part of a tween relationship:

- More than half, or 59%, know that their child has kissed a boyfriend or girlfriend.

- Almost one in five, or seventeen percent, knows their child has made out with a partner.

- Only seven percent say their child has gone further than kissing or making out.

Dating Relationships in Tweens Begin Much Earlier Than Adults Realize

Remember, we're only talking about tweens (not teens), so when it comes to sexual relationships, you might be surprised to know:

- 47% of tweens in general and 37% of age 11 - 12 say they've been in a boyfriend and girlfriend relationship.

- 72% say dating relationships begin by age fourteen.

- The main rise in the teen pregnancy rate is among girls younger than fifteen.

Nearly One-Third of Tweens and Parents Say Sexual Activity is a Part of Tween Dating Relationships

Specifically, the percentage of tweens identified below acknowledge the following acts as part of a dating relationship:

- Regarding touching and feeling, up to 37% of tweens considered it acceptable, and as many as 31% of the parents also considered it acceptable.

- When it came to oral sex as many as 27% of tweens considered it acceptable, and as many as 26% of the parents also considered it acceptable.

- And last but not least, when it came to sexual intercourse as many as 28% of tweens considered it acceptable and as many as 26% of the parents also considered it acceptable.

Tweens in Relationships Report Sexual Activity Among Their Peer Group

If these shock and awe statistics below don't already frighten you, they should by now.

- Within their peer group, 47% of tweens know a friend or someone their age who has touched and felt up a partner.

- Up to 31% of tweens know a friend or peer who has had oral sex.

- And one third, 33% know a friend or peer who has had sexual intercourse!

Adolescents Who Date Early Are Twice as Likely to Develop Behavioral Problems

Even more cause for concern is a recent Canadian research study, as reported by the Wall Street Journal, which suggests boys and girls who start dating at a young age may disrupt the typical pattern of romantic development and increase their risk of school and behavioral problems.

A corroborating report by the Journal of Adolescence studied young romance and looked at groups of children who started dating at the average age of 11.6 years, as compared to 12.9 for "on-time teens" and an average age of 14.9 for the so-called "late bloomers." Twenty percent of the participants had started dating as young as ages 10 - 12, while 25% began in their late teens.

Those who started dating early were twice as likely to develop behavioral problems as compared to those who began "on-time" or later in adolescence. Lying, cheating, truancy, picking fights and running away constituted disruptive behaviors. Early starting children were also more likely to report personality traits such as shyness, depression, and aggression.

Meanwhile, late-blooming children experienced an accelerated path towards exclusive relationships from casual dating with no adverse effects. About 55% of participants were classified as "on-time" teens.

Why might early relationships be detrimental to tweens and teens? Researchers concluded that when entering a relationship early on when ill-prepared and without the appropriate support of peers, adolescents may have more difficulty dealing with the stress of a typical couple. Early-starters were also found to be more likely to drink alcohol and engage in unsafe sex.

Tweens Are Not Emotionally and/or Physically Mature Enough for a Romantic Relationship

The two mentioned studies bring up two good points: 1) tweens are not in a good position to be early daters because they typically don't possess healthy relationship skills, and 2) any tween who wants to begin a relationship should have healthy relationship skills and know how to recognize them in a prospective candidate. Otherwise, entering a tween romance can be disastrous. A tween, and any teen, who wants to enter a serious romantic relationship should have the following four skills:

- Assertiveness.
- Problem-solving.
- Emotion regulation.
- Conflict resolution.

Do most tweens, whose ages range from 10 - 12, possess this skill set? The answer is no, they don't, and that's why they shouldn't be engaged in any kind of romantic relationship. Is a friend's/plutonic only relationship, acceptable such as on a group date? With proper adult supervision where there is no physical contact, yes it can be.

Set Realistic Dating Expectations for Tweens Early On

Whatever your personal rules are about dating, it's important to make this a discussion that you regularly have with your daughter. Explain the reasoning behind your rules and let her know that you understand her frustration and her urge to grow up. Say something like, "I know you really want to go on dates like the other girls your age but dating before you're ready can have negative consequences. You have your whole life to enjoy dating. Enjoy being young and hanging out with your friends."

The bottom line is that parents must be vigilant about safe and sane dating habits. You want your daughter to feel comfortable coming to you with questions and concerns regarding dating. Keep the lines of communication open and let her know that there is no topic too big or scary for you to tackle as a family. Dating can be difficult enough as it is but dating when you're eleven-years old can be downright overwhelming and destructive. Encourage your daughter to enjoy her age and freedom rather than making her primary focus all about dating.

Do most teenagers, whose ages range from 13 - 18, possess the four skill sets previously noted? The answer varies and can be yes, or no, or somewhere in between. All tweens and teens are unique, and these variables will be discussed in more detail in the next section.

Teen Dating Basics

If you haven't already done so, give your children the "big talk" about sex. They need to know how their body is changing, and exactly what happens in the physical act of sex. They need to hear this from you. Don't let them hear only what their friends say about it. This is the perfect time to tell them before they start dating. They're seeing the physical signs, and they still look up to you and your opinions. Make sure the talk is not all straight facts. Add in your opinion on love and relationships in your own terms and with your own personal stories if possible.

And then ask them this question; "What's the purpose of dating?'

There are many answers to this question; however, three basic purposes can be summed up as follows:

- ➢ Practice or friendship.
- ➢ Love and romance.
- ➢ Marriage and children.

Your daughter's response, if she has one, will usually fall into one of these categories, or straddle two of them.

Dating for Practice or Friendship

Nowadays teens scramble to get dates to school dances and proms purely as a form of plumage, proof that one isn't a social pariah. Many teens go to school dances with people with whom they had no sexual relations with and there is no romantic interest involved. Welcome to the twenty-first century!

Dating for Love and Romance

Love and romance sounds wonderful but like everything else in life, it has its ups and downs. Falling in love means there's always the possibility of falling out of love, or having your heart broken. It may not seem like a big deal if it's never happened to you, but for someone that it has, there are many complicated problems and difficult emotions to deal with when love goes wrong or ends abruptly.

Dating for Marriage and Children

If the purpose of dating is to marry and eventually have children, but you're too young to marry, then one point of view is that you're too young to date. The only repercussion of this dating category is perhaps a broken heart. If you date too long, even if you sincerely love each other, you open yourself up to a lot of temptation. All those legitimate feelings have nowhere to go, because you can't marry yet.

Teen dating can be thought of as a training ground and there is a natural progression from friendship, to love and sex, and to marriage (or marriage first and then sex after). To get to that point from an immature child to a mature adult, takes time and many steps in development, preferably one at a time.

The driver's license analogy is a good one in regard to dating because before you can get your driver's license (substitute that license for a marriage license) you need a learner's permit to practice, and before you practice you need a car to drive in, and to pass the driver's test you need to master control of the car and obey the rules of the road. Right?

Shock and Awe Teenage Dating Statistics No Parent Can Ignore!

Teens are exposed to intimate relationships early on, so before your teen starts dating, sit down with them and make sure they're aware of these ten thought provoking facts. Then ask them what they think about them before they start dating. Did any of them grab their attention? If so, why?

- Statistics show that 46% of teens between the ages of 15 - 19 have had sex at least once.

- 67% of teens who have had sex wish that they had waited (60% of boys and 77% of girls).

- Despite declines in rates of teen pregnancy in the U.S., about 820,000 teens become pregnant each year. That means that 34% of teenagers have at least one pregnancy before they turn twenty!

- Nearly four in ten teenage girls whose first intercourse experience happened at thirteen or fourteen reports that the sex was unwanted or involuntary.

- A teenager who is having unprotected sex has a 90% change of becoming pregnant within a year.

> Approximately one in five high school girls has been physically or sexually abused in some way or form by a dating partner.

If these statistics got their attention, it's time for the big sex talk about dating or a follow-up one. The more the better! How to talk to your daughter about sex will be covered in more detail in Chapter 2: Preparing Your Daughter for Dating. In the meantime, if having "the big talk" with your child makes you nervous; Dr. Phil offers the following general advice below.

How to Talk to Your Daughter About Sex

The hardest part in talking to your child about sex is getting started. The big talk needs to start early, because you want to keep an open dialog with your child from early childhood on. You also want to be able to talk about sex and dating with them, while they still listen to you. And when I say early, I mean before middle school, preferably from the fourth, fifth, and sixth grades depending on their stage of development. Most attractions start about middle school, and with it the pressure to have sex begins.

It's important your daughter has a clear concept of what you expect from her and what they can expect from dating, because they really do look for boundaries. So, what you're doing when you have these discussions with them is laying out what's acceptable behavior and what's not acceptable behavior. Theorist and psychology both agree that most teens have their values formed by the time they're twelve, so don't wait until then to have the big talk.

Does Your Teen Have Healthy Relationship Skills?

A teen who wants to enter a serious romantic relationship should have the four skill sets listed below. As adults and parents, most of us still struggle with mastering these skills so imagine how much more difficult it can be for an adolescent to master them as well. Most of us, whether we're an adult, adolescent or child, don't get it right the first time. Sometimes it takes a second, or a third time, and so on. Mastering these skills is a never-ending process, because even as adults, so few of us ever get it right, let alone the first time.

Assertiveness Skills

Sometimes relationships come with a lot of pressure. Dating teens may feel the pressure to become sexually active when they spend a lot of time together. It's important for your teen to be able to speak up for herself so she can say no when she's feeling uncomfortable.

Problem Solving Skills

A romantic relationship will create different types of problems that your teen may not have experienced before. For example, a teen may have to decide whether to spend time with a friend or a boyfriend or she may need to resolve problems that result from a misunderstanding over social media.

Emotion Regulation Skills

The teen years can be tumultuous by nature, and romance certainly stirs up a lot of intense emotions. It's important for any teen to be able to deal with stress, loneliness, anger, jealousy, and sadness in a healthy manner.

Conflict Resolution Skills

A relationship will likely bring some level of conflict, whether it's a disagreement about a miscommunication or an argument over how the other person is behaving. It's important for your teen to understand how to resolve conflict in a healthy way.

Does Your Teen Understand Healthy Relationships?

Teens also need to know what a healthy relationship should look like. As a parent, if you haven't role modeled healthy relationships, it's likely that your teen's view of what a healthy relationship is may be unclear. But even teens who have witnessed healthy relationships may not understand themselves how to create a healthy dating relationship.

Make sure your daughter understands issues, like dating violence, and jealousy. Talk to her about the importance of maintaining healthy relationships with her friends even while dating someone. It's also important for your teen to be willing to remain involved in school work and extra-curricular activities without allowing a romantic interest to interfere. That's a must!

Has Your Teen Had Plenty of Education About Dating and Sexuality?

Make sure your teen has a clear understanding of dating and sexuality issues. Your teen should know what to expect when entering a romantic relationship and to understand the dangers of engaging in sexual activity, like STDs and pregnancy. Even a teen who insists she's not ready to have sex, should still understand the potential consequences. Better safe than sorry!

Don't expect your kid's school system to teach tweens and teens everything they need to know about sex, intimacy, and dating. There is no one standard sex education curriculum in the USA and every state has the choice of using a "comprehensive" or "abstinence" curriculum, or combinations of each.

Does Your Teen Have a Healthy Sense of Self Worth?

For most daughters entering their teen years is an exciting, confusing, and a crazy time to be in. Emotions can be all over the place, and it can feel like the whole world is trying to press her into their mold instead of letting her be who she wants to be. If your teen hasn't yet established a healthy self-worth, it could be dangerous for her to enter a relationship.

If your daughter doesn't feel good about herself or hasn't yet established a healthy identity, she may tie her self-worth into the person she's dating. She may seek attention to feel good about herself or may be willing to tolerate unhealthy behavior.

It's important to have ongoing conversations with your teen about dating, relationships, and sexuality. If you forbid dating of any kind, your teen may rebel and begin dating without your knowledge. Try to allow your teen some freedom but make sure you keep your teen safe by establishing healthy dating rules.

We'll explore more about what these healthy dating rules are in Chapter 3: Best Dating Practices for Your Daughter. But first, let's discuss why every daughter deserves a gentleman in the next chapter.

2 – Preparing Your Daughter for Dating

Dating is a big part of a teenage girl's life and every girl dreams of going out on that first date or going to a special place with a special guy. However, dating is not always easy for teenage girls. As the matter of fact, it can be one of the most difficult parts of being a teenager.

Teen dating is a minefield of emotions and hormones, which may lead to conflict and disharmony in the family household if not carefully managed. Parents cannot bury their head in the sand and ignore what's happening. They should empower their children to make the right decisions by offering limitless love and support.

If you want this whole dating thing to turn out for the best, it's going to require some extra effort for dad and daughter. And mom's too! The more you're involved and proactive in the dating process as a chaperone, date planner, ride service, confidant, mentor, or whatever, the more you'll be in control in this new adventure for your daughter.

Smart Parents Empower Their Teens for Teenage Dating

Smart parents empower their teens to become educated about dating, rather than avoid the entire issue. In their teenage years, your children will be discovering a lot about their bodies and emotions, and as an effective parent, you need to support and guide them through this process to help them avoid making costly mistakes.

Some parents may feel that this is smothering their children or interfering in their teenager's lives. Other parents, unable to confront the issues, may go into denial and try to ban their teens from dating at all. It's the smart parents who confront the issues head on, working with their children and empowering them to make the right decisions. Good parents can help protect their teens from the pitfalls of dating.

Dating is a Time of Social Experimentation for Teens

A daughter's adolescent years are a time to test out which type of partners appeal to them, and how they can negotiate a romantic relationship. It can also be a confusing and difficult time for parents too. "Today" show contributor Dr. Gail Saltz, a psychiatrist with New York Presbyterian Hospital, has some advice below.

First Date Tips for Daughters, Candidates, and Supervising Parents

Teen dating can be a challenging time where self-confidence is built up, and dating techniques are learned. Teens also learn how to be both assertive and compromising, how to be giving to another and how to expect the same in return. All of this is sort of a practice session in order to find "Mr. Right." But that's no reason not to try. An important part of teenage dating is starting when they're physically and emotionally mature enough to do it safely and sanely and having good role models.

Be a Good Role Model

A parent's relationship with their partner is a model for how your teen will behave with others, and your relationship with your child speaks far louder than anyone's words. Show them how you compromise, stick up for yourself, give and get respect, argue and compromise and love your spouse. Parents need to lead by example for their teenagers to look up to when it comes to responsible dating and healthy relationships.

Tell Her to Listen to Her Inner Voice

Help her pay attention to her inner voice that says, "I'm uncomfortable in this situation and don't want to do this." Teach her to trust her better judgment. Tell her how to avoid unwanted sexual advances. Tell her that any boy who claims to be a man because he's had sex is not a man. The title of manhood comes with all sorts of responsibilities that only come later in life as a young and responsible adult. Tell your daughters that having sex doesn't automatically make her a woman either.

Warn Her About the Danger Signs

Being manipulated, verbally put down, pushed or slapped and kept isolated from other relationships are all signs of an abusive relationship. Make sure your daughter understands that she can come to you or another parent/teacher/counselor if they feel threatened, conflicted, or oppressed by her boyfriend.

No Means No!

Remind her she needs to be honest and clear in communication. "I'm not sure…" from a girl can mean "I just need to be pushed or pressured some more before I say yes" to her date. Teach her to say "No" clearly and firmly. Candidates need to know that if they hear "No" and they proceed anyway, it's date rape!

Don't allow any inappropriate touching. This is a given and be reminded that tweens are notorious for 'wrestling' but are still children at heart and might still play games with the opposite sex that are no longer appropriate. Point these times out as they come along, without getting angry.

Resist Pressure to Have Sex

Everybody matures at different rates and at different times. For many teens, there's pressure to have sex at an early age. Smart parents are aware of the way in which society has progressed and embraced an open, honest and sincere relationship with their teens when it comes to the subject of sex. You should too!

Empowered, informed and educated teens understand the issues of sex and the associated risks of pre-marital sex and are in a much better position to make the right decision for themselves. Modern sex education, if it's taught, covers a broad range of topics that can help teens feel in control of their actions and take responsibility for them.

It's Ok to Get Their Heart Broken

Nobody can teach teens how to avoid having their heart broken. Indeed, many would argue that one of life's lessons is having your heart broken for the first time. That doesn't mean teens should be left to deal with such heartaches without support. Parents should encourage their teens to be respectful and honest with others, and to express their feelings sincerely. Parents should create an environment where their teens think about others and look after one another in social situations.

Of course, this won't guarantee your daughter won't get her heart broken, but it will ensure she's respected by her peers and partners, and she can help create the right environment by engaging in healthy relationships. Helping teens demonstrate the right behavior ensures they understand what they should expect from others and helps them more easily identify the right people to date.

Avoid Abusive Relationships

The group Teens Experiencing Abusive Relationships (TEAR) reports that one in three teenagers knows a friend who "has been hit, punched, kicked, slapped, choked or physically hurt by their partner." This shocking statistic highlights the issue of abuse in teen relationships and illustrates the scale of the problem. Abuse in any relationship is a serious issue, but teens have specific issues due to the changes in their bodies and emotions, and peer pressure to behave in a certain way.

Part of the problem with teen abuse is that some teens feel they can't confide in anybody. Smart parents maintain an open dialogue, approaching their teens, taking time to talk honestly and calmly with them, and creating a nonjudgmental, supportive environment. Many teens are simply unaware of the warning signs that may indicate the potential for a boyfriend (or daughter) to be abusive. Parents can provide an objective viewpoint, not by policing their teens' activities but by encouraging them to talk about how they feel.

Start Having the Sex Talks

Adolescence is a time for learning. And learning about intimate relationships during their tween and teen years is what helps them prepare for adult relationships. So, by all means, be open, understanding, and compassionate with your teen, and do give them the "talk" about sex as many times as needed.

Your daughter needs to know her body is changing, and exactly what happens in the physical act of sex. She needs to hear this from you and not what her friends say about it. The perfect time to tell her is before she sees the first signs of her body changing and starts puberty, your daughter will still look up to you and respect your opinions. Make sure the talk is not all straight facts. Put in your opinion on love and relationships as well as your own personal stories.

The Same-Sex Parent Should Have the Discussion

Although dads can be supportive of their daughters as they go through puberty and may want to be involved in the big talk, this is something that mothers should be primarily responsible for. "At this point, she is noticing the differences between guys and girls," Dr. Phil explains, "and so she's going to feel uncomfortable with dad being there." Nonetheless, dad can be available for moral support, but moms should do the heavy lifting for this discussion.

It's OK to Feel Embarrassed

The hardest part in talking to your child about sex is getting started. "What you need to do first is get straight in your mind that 'This is something I have to do,'" Dr. Phil says. It's natural to feel embarrassed at first. Just work through the fear. If need be, have a sense of humor about it. "You can laugh about being nervous and say, 'My mom never talked to me about this,'" Dr. Phil explains. Letting your daughter know that you're a bit shy about the subject matter may help to let her guard down.

Start with the Mechanics and be Anatomically Correct

As your daughter develops secondary sexual characteristics, like breasts and pubic hair, she may ask questions like "Why do I need a bra?" or "When will I get my period?" Dr. Phil says it's a great idea to find a book that has anatomically correct drawings of the reproductive systems to illustrate what's going on in her body. "Explain what happens when she has a period, so she's not freaked out when it happens," Dr. Phil advises. "Let her know what to expect. Tell her how to be prepared for it, go through all of those things with her." Use pictures to back up your facts.

Discuss Sex in the Context of a Loving, Mature Relationship

After you've discussed the mechanics with your daughter, hopefully in the same conversation, you need to talk about sex. "The important thing when you talk about sex is that you don't say that this is anything other than healthy and normal," Dr. Phil says. "But you need to explain that this is something that has to be framed in a relationship after you've grown up and there's love and commitment and a history and an understanding that you have to be responsible with your body." The main thing you want is for your daughter to come away from your discussion saying, 'I now have some accurate information, and my mother has told me that I need to really respect and protect my body.'"

Discuss Age Appropriate Topics

How much information is too much for your daughter to handle? If you're unsure, use her questions as a barometer of what to talk about. "It would be very unusual for a 9-year-old to ask a question about orgasm," Dr. Phil says. "So don't go there at this point. You don't want to give her information that she doesn't have the constructs or the concepts to deal with. You can be very global, and you can be very abstract about it at this point." Ask for her questions, then come back and discuss it in a week. Remember to keep the lines of communication open.

Change the Context of Your Talk

If you sit your daughter down on the couch, look her squarely in the eye and say, "We need to talk about sex," she may hit the floor. Try changing the context of your talk so it doesn't seem so ominous. "Sometimes it's easier if you're driving down the street, where they can kind of look out the window," Dr. Phil suggests. If you make the environment of your chat disarming, your daughter won't feel quite put on the spot and so conspicuous.

What Constitutes Sex?

First tell her she shouldn't be having sex yet and that there are too many risks involved. You hope she'll follow this advice and wait to have sex when she's married, a young adult, or mature enough to handle the responsibility. But don't count on it!

It's best to educate her early, have the sex talk, and inform her about contraception, unprotected sex, and sexually transmitted diseases. Encourage your daughter to think seriously about what sexual intimacy means to her. Advise her that her partner is not allowed a million different ways to have sex with her. Tell her she doesn't need to have sex to keep a partner. And don't forget to remind her that oral sex and anal sex are sex. Many kids think otherwise and tell themselves it's not really sex.

First Date Tips for Teen Girls

Teenage girls are often shy and nervous prior to a first date and look forward to their first date with a mixture of emotions. By preparing her for that important step, you can help ease your daughter's anxiety so that her first date will be an enjoyable experience. A few simple tips below can lessen her jitters and help ease her into dating so eventually she knows what to do on her own.

Daddy Daughter Dates

As a dad, one annual date and rite of passage you don't want to miss is the daddy-daughter dance presented by your school, church, or other organization. Here's the point. The primary purpose of dating your daughter is making memories and cementing your lifetime connection. But there's another huge benefit to showing up on time, opening her car door, treating her with respect, and handling any mishaps with grace and a smile as an "acceptable" candidate. You're modeling for your daughter the way any boy should act when she goes out on any date at any time.

Think about it! When some "unacceptable candidate" takes her out, she won't put up with any nonsense because her dad taught her how a gentleman acts on a date. Don't lose this golden opportunity to show her in person how a gentleman treats a lady and behaves on a date.

Finally, when your daughter does start dating boys her own age, that doesn't mean your dates with her should end. That's another reason you want to spend more time with her, not less. You may have to work a little harder at it to get on her busy social calendar, but if you ask nicely, she just might fit you in. Oh yeah dad, don't forget to keep dating your wife, too!

Time for a Real Date with an Acceptable Candidate

Encourage your daughter to remember that dating comes with mixed emotions. She might be nervous, happy, and afraid, to name a few. Like any new experience in life she must take it one step at a time. If her first date doesn't go well like most first dates do not to worry! The first boy she dates will most likely never be the one she marries so tell her to have fun, don't worry about making mistakes, and enjoy herself. It won't be perfect!

If your daughter gets nervous about asking someone out on a date, let her know that she's not alone. Many, if not most, teens have anxious feelings when they ask someone out on a date because they open themselves up for rejection and that can be a blow to their self-esteem. But that's no reason not to try. Regardless of who asks who for a date here's some great advice before it happens.

Preparation

Your daughter should decide on a day and time for her date, that is agreeable to her and the candidate, to first introduce himself to her parents. This will help ease your daughter's nerves and yours as well, but not necessarily his, before the first date.

A proper introduction is very important so that the parents, preferably both, know who he is, where the two of them are going, and what time they'll be back. For a more thorough overview of the do's and don'ts on this topic, read Chapter 6: Meeting the Parents and the Candidate Interview.

Your daughter should allow enough time before the date to dress in her favorite clothes and apply her appropriate makeup. Let her know when she's done that she looks beautiful. Don't allow her on the other hand try to dress the way she thinks her date would like her to dress. If she feels uncomfortable or unnatural about this, it will reflect in her attitude. If she feels comfortable with herself and can be herself, it will most likely be a better date.

Physical Involvement

Set ground rules for physical involvement ahead of time with your daughter. She won't be able to think clearly when her hormones are raging. She needs to know that no candidate can pressure her with unwanted advances. Especially on first dates, she doesn't need the added stress that physical intimacy places on a relationship.

Regarding physical intimacy, restrictions and limits should be set by each family based on their values. Affectionate touching such as holding hands, a pat on the shoulder, or perhaps a good-night kiss, should be the limit of her physical involvement on first dates. Once again, depending on your family values.

Communication

Your daughter should practice effective communication techniques on a date. She should be friendly, talk about herself and interests, but make sure she listens to him as well. Listening will help her discover what she does or doesn't like about him and will help her with further qualities to look for in future candidates.

If he's evasive, rude or makes continued sexual comments, your daughter needs to know that this type of candidate is someone she should never date again. Make sure she's not too flirty, pushy or fake. She must be herself and not what he wants her to be. He should accept her for who she is and nothing more.

Respect

Your daughter should also be respectful to her date. He has feelings and may be just as unsure of himself and nervous on a first date as she is. Respect and trust are two-way streets, and she needs to treat him politely as well. If he's rude or crude, question if he's ready to date, or at least he's the right choice for a date. She needs to think highly of herself, so she never settles for anything less than the best treatment from her date.

What Matters Most in Finding the Right Candidate

To find out what's important to your daughter in a dating candidate, ask her if she's interested in creating two lists. The first list is titled "I Want a Boyfriend Who…?" list. It will help her sort out what she wants in a boyfriend. The second list is titled "I Don't Want a Boyfriend Who….?"

A Father's Rulebook on the Do's and Don'ts for Dating His Little Princess

Tell her not to focus on appearance when she's making these two lists, and instead, think about personal qualities or strengths she admires in people. Once she has a clearer image of the characteristics she's looking for, it's easier to recognize a potential match as well as avoid relationships that have little chance of working out.

The first thing you can do is make a mental or written list of all the attributes that you as a parent consider a prerequisite for dating your daughter. At the same time, make another list of those characteristics that will not be tolerated. For the most part, this list should comprise all the negative attributes regarding the worst possible and the least desirable candidates. If you're not sure, skip ahead to Chapters 18 and 19.

Regarding the positive qualities she's looking for in a boyfriend, they can be about personality traits, values, or anything else. Your lists should be private, so don't hold back! The more detailed you make it, the better. You might be really surprised by some of your answers. Make the lists as long and as specific as you can, until you run out of ideas.

Now compare them side by side and see if they are one and the same. If they're not the same, discuss why not. After a while, your lists might look like this:

I Want a Boyfriend Who…?

- Is available and wants a relationship with me.
- Is intelligent.
- Has a good sense of humor.
- Is friendly.
- Cares about his looks but doesn't obsess over them.

I Don't Want a Boyfriend Who….?

- Has a bad temper.

- Is into drugs or alcohol.
- Acts jealous.
- Is conceited.
- Is a total slob.

She should review her list to see if any of her wants are vague. If she wrote, "I want a boyfriend who's nice," she's not being specific. What exactly does "nice" mean to her? Does it mean her boyfriend calls her every night? Never breaks dates? Gives her gifts on special occasions? She needs to be specific and elaborate on her needs and then eliminate the vague statements.

Everything on her list isn't equally important. Some items rate as "This is a must!" Others are in the "Would be good but not essential" category. For example, if she insists her boyfriend to be athletic, mark that item "This is a must!" If she thinks it would be cool to be involved with someone who's into the same music as she is, mark that item "Would be good but not essential."

When she's done, does her list describe anybody she already knows? Someone you're ok with her dating? Great! This sounds like an acceptable candidate and she's ready for her first date.

3 – Best Dates and Practices for Your Daughter

Regarding the term "dating," it can mean many different things under many different circumstances. For tweens it could mean a "group" date where many tweens of both sexes who are merely friends (plutonic relationships) meet at a local theatre to watch a movie together. Or for older teens it could mean a "single" date between two teenage lovers having a romantic dinner on the town all by themselves.

No matter what kind of date it is, having a dating age daughter can be a sour dose of reality to swallow for most dads. Wouldn't it be awesome if there was some way to turn back her biological clock or hold it steady? Ban all contact? Or just forbid her to date forever? As dads, these are some of the thoughts that cross our minds and questions we ask ourselves and as we come to the realization that our daughters are growing up quicker than we expected and are maturing into tweens, teens, and young women.

Once a parent has accepted the inevitable, and believe their daughter is ready to start dating, the end goal is for her to choose and/or accept a candidate of character, preferably a gentleman. However, if every teenage daughter deserves a gentleman, then every teenage candidate deserves a lady as well. They both go hand in hand. How one behaves around the opposite sex is often determined by which roles they play. Gentleman and lady, or player and slut. There is only one acceptable choice!

Nonetheless, there are all sorts of candidates out there of every character type and intent. Of every possible race, creed, color, religion and social status. None of the latter qualities should matter, only the former ones, as they matter most. What really matters is the content of the character of the candidate, attitude about dating, respect for the opposite sex, and how honorable his intentions are with your daughter.

What is a Gentleman These Days?

Good question! The American Heritage College Dictionary describes a **gentleman** as: "A well-mannered and considerate man with high standards of proper behavior." That one sentence is paramount to this section and sums up what every dad expects from each and every candidate, without fail, or dereliction of duty.

Another more descriptive account of what a gentleman stands for is below and it has stood the test of time:

"The True Gentleman is the man whose conduct proceeds from good will and an acute sense of propriety, and whose self-control is equal to all emergencies; who does not make the poor man conscious of his poverty, the obscure man of his obscurity, or any man of his inferiority or deformity; who is himself humbled if necessity compels him to humble another; who does not flatter wealth, cringe before power, or boast of his own possessions or achievements; who speaks with frankness but always with sincerity and sympathy; whose deed follows his word; who thinks of the rights and feelings of others, rather than his own; and who appears well in any company, a man with whom honor is sacred and virtue safe."

John Walter Wayland (Virginia 1899)

Semper Fidelis is Latin for or "Always Faithful" and is well known in the United States as the motto of the U.S. Marine Corps where it is often shortened to Semper Fi. It too is another term that can be applied to the dating process because it's what we expect of every candidate to be when they are dating our daughters. Always faithful!

Always faithful as in what is in the best interest of our daughters and always faithful to being a gentleman at all times and not just when it suits his best interest. Being faithful occurs rain or shine, night and day, 24/7 and 365 days a year with no holidays in between for excuses.

Another ideal quality of a candidate is to be chivalrous. Chivalry is the combination of qualities expected of an ideal knight, especially courage, honor, justice, and a readiness to help the weak. The best quality in today's age, as it was then, is to be courteous in behavior, especially towards women, but to others as well, regardless of their sex or orientation.

Character Counts

Character counts and applies to every candidate. There are seven ethical values, Seven Pillars if you will, that everyone can agree on. The Seven Pillars of Character is an adaptation from the Six Pillars Program by Character Counts, with the seventh pillar of Sapience added.

Please note these values are not political, religious, or culturally biased. They are universal and can be applied to anyone, and in particular, they apply to gentlemen and ladies. Use the points in each pillar to evaluate your daughter's dating choices and their character as follows.

Trustworthiness

Be honest • Don't deceive, cheat, or steal • Be reliable, do what you say you'll do • Have the courage to do the right thing • Build a good reputation • Be loyal, stand by your family, friends, and country

Respect

Treat others with respect; follow the Golden Rule • Be tolerant and accepting of differences • Use good manners, not bad language • Be considerate of the feelings of others • Don't threaten, hit or hurt anyone • Deal peacefully with anger, insults, and disagreements

Responsibility

Do what you're supposed to do • Plan ahead • Persevere: keep on trying! • Always do your best • Use self-control • Be self-disciplined • Think before you act, consider the consequences • Be accountable for your words, actions, and attitudes

Fairness

Play by the rules • Take turns and share • Be open-minded; listen to others • Don't take advantage of others • Don't blame others carelessly • Treat all people fairly

Caring

Be kind • Be compassionate and show you care • Express gratitude • Forgive others • Help people in need • Empathize with others

Citizenship

Make your school and community better • Cooperate • Stay informed; vote • Be a good neighbor • Obey laws and rules • Respect authority • Protect the environment • Volunteer

Sapience

Be a person of/or showing great wisdom and sound judgment • Take action to advance society with personal intelligence and enlightenment • Work now and together with others; to make the world a better place

Eighteen Gentlemanly Traditions That Still Apply Today

Chivalry is dead when the gentleman no longer understands the meaning behind his chivalrous acts. When actions no longer come from within, but are forced and non-genuine, the inner gentleman dies and so does chivalry.

Being a gentleman is the highest calling a candidate can have. It's expected of each and every candidate to follow the gentleman's code of honor. To help encourage these virtues, eighteen of the best traditions are listed below to follow along with the reasons and history behind a gentleman's etiquette.

1.   He stands when she walks in the room

In the old days, men stood out of respect when a lady, dignitary, or elderly person walked in the room. It was a sign of respect and humbleness. Today, men stand out of courtesy when a guest visits a meeting. A gentleman will stand from his table when he's introduced to a guest. Standing for her shows you're attentive and you care.

2.   He walks by her on the outside, closest to the street

Why is the top coat symbolic of the gentleman? Before our drainage systems came to be, a man stood on the outside of the sidewalk in a long coat to protect her from the dust and sewage that could splash up as horse carriages passed by. Sewage was common in the streets. The picture of the man laying his coat over a puddle for her to walk over meant he was protecting her feet from fecal material more so than rain water.

Today, a gentleman might stand in the way of puddles splashing up from buses, or in the event a car veers onto the sidewalk. Symbolically it might mean he'll always be by her side, through thick and thin, and will protect her from anything.

3.   He opens the door for her

A gentleman would help her up into the carriage as a sign of his protection and strength. Women would hold their dresses up as they were often long and heavy. The gentleman opened the door for her, so she wouldn't have to drop her dress in the dirt. The modern gentleman helps her in and out of the car to stand in the way of creepy gawkers. Opening a door for her is not a sign she is weak, but a gesture of affection.

4. He pulls out her chair

It was common for the gentleman to pull out her chair and allow her to face the open room. Today, the gentleman pulls out her seat, and sits facing her and away from the bar, TV, and crowd because he doesn't want to be distracted from his priority which is her and only her.

5. He sits after she sits

At the table he waits until she is seated and waits until every lady is seated, before taking his own place. Talk show hosts continue this tradition today by waiting to sit until after their guest has taken their seat. If Oprah does it, so can you if she's your guest. Allow her to sit first.

6. He helps her put on/take off her coat

Up through the Victorian age, women wore multiple layers, and beneath them a restricting corset. A gentleman would help his lady put on and take off her coat because of her restricted movement. Corsets are not common today, but many women still enjoy the help of a gentleman can give them when slipping on their coat or jacket, so he can block the view with his body.

7. He doesn't walk ahead of her

Because ladies wore long dresses and could trip on them, the gentleman walked behind her when climbing a staircase. Tumbling down a flight of stairs isn't a good way to end a date. Today, the gentleman follows this etiquette rule because she might be wearing long heels or a long dress. This is another sign of him protecting her. However, she may want him to walk upstairs first if she's wearing a short skirt.

8. He gives up his seat to her if there is only standing room

A gentleman offers his seat to a lady if there are no other seats on the bus/train or a busy restaurant, coffee house, or classroom.

9.   He carries her bags

A gentleman will help her carry her bags today, and when flying, will assist others in putting their luggage in the overhead compartments.

10.   He picks up the check

Still today, the gentleman picks up the tab, especially on the first date, and with no expectations. Ladies can amend the rule after the first date if they so choose to.

11.   He holds an umbrella over her when it rains

It was common for a younger person to hold an umbrella for an older person. When it rains, the gentleman holds an umbrella over her and doesn't mind getting a little wet.

12.   He gives her his jacket

A gentleman pays attention, and if he notices her shivering, he gives her his jacket to wear to keep her warm.

13.   He keeps her secrets

A gentleman will always keep a secret, especially the one entrusted to him by the woman of his dreams. Should a break-up happen, the gentleman can still be trusted to keep it his own.

14.   He walks her home or to safety

A true gentleman will walk her to her car or home to this day because he's concerned for her safety.

15. *He listens to her*

To be a good listener is as indispensable as good manners. A gentleman always listens because he wants to get to know her on a deeper level.

16. *He's on time*

A gentleman is his word. Traffic is not an excuse for being late to a date (unless a sig-alert). A good man plans in advance. Don't keep her waiting.

17. *He compliments her*

She spent a lot of time getting ready, so a gentleman always compliments. He doesn't play on her insecurities.

18. *He would never dream of manhandling or hitting any woman*

A gentleman finds no excuse to hit a woman, no matter what.

Attitude, Appearance and Attire

It's common to expect most people to treat you as you appear and how you are dressed. People are judged by others by their attitude and clothes and first impression. It may not be fair, and it may not be right, but in the real world our all too visible self is under constant scrutiny. Below is a quick contrast of acceptable examples of attitude, appearance, and attire, and unacceptable ones.

- Unacceptable saggin' pants **versus** acceptable pulled-up slacks or jeans.

- Unacceptable gangsta' hoody look **versus** acceptable baseball cap.

- Unacceptable slouching and poor posture **versus** acceptable erect and attentive posture.

A Father's Rulebook on the Do's and Don'ts for Dating His Little Princess

- Unacceptable gang signs and visible tattoos **versus** non-offensive attire and no visible tattoos.

- Unacceptable open shirt and excessive bling **versus** button-up shirt and modest jewelry.

- Unacceptable hand gestures and body language **versus** acceptable body language and facial gestures.

- Unacceptable messy and disorderly attire **versus**. orderly and neat attire.

As part of this book's commitment to ensuring that every daughter dates a gentleman, the publisher Fratire Publishing produced a YouTube video, a public service announcement or sorts showing ten "unacceptable" dating candidates meeting their date's father at the front door and because every daughter deserves a gentleman, are turned away at the door, each stinging with rejection.

In the second half of the video, all ten dating candidates return with better attitude, appearance, and attire as "acceptable" dating candidates and are warmly greeted by the father and welcomed through the front door.

As a dating candidate, would you pass this test? Find out for yourself in the Appendix under the title of the YouTube Video: "So You Want to Date My Daughter? A Father's Rulebook on the Do's and Don'ts for Dating His Little Princess."

Worse yet, if you want to see a 1:56 minute video documentary of un-gentlemanly (bad boy) behavior in action towards one woman who experiences 100 catcalls during a ten-hour period as she walked around New York City, check out the YouTube video in the Appendix with link titled: "Watch This Woman Receive 100 Catcalls While Walking Around for a Day."

The Bad Boy Syndrome

Guess what? Preteen, teenage girls, and even young women are attracted to bad boys!

Why is that you ask? Why is it that so many good girls go bad? Is it that young girls only see the frosting on top and not what's rotten underneath? Is it because tweens and teens don't make the best of choices because they haven't had enough of life's experiences to tell them what may seem like "Mr. Right" can easily turn out to be "Mr. Wrong."

This type of candidate is commonly known as a Bad Boy, a Player, Playboy, Rico Suave, etc. and most bad boys only want one thing, to have sex and they will say and do most anything to get it, and they must be avoided at all costs!

This is a wake-up call for every dad and parent to educate their daughter on all the signs of a bad boyfriend or date. Let her know that she can talk to you about anything including what she finds appealing. Let her know that she needs to be able to recognize the signs of a bad boy and bad boy syndrome before she gets seriously involved with him.

Do you remember what bad boys used to look or act like? Think of John Travolta's character in "Grease." He's an iconic bad boy with a few good traits as well. Women used to swoon over his image. Many still do. But if you look at it objectively (which might be difficult if you love the movie as I do), you will see that his character had a lot of horrible, dangerous habits, a problem with anger/violence, and he was a shallow womanizer. A lot of modern bad boys still fit these criteria. So what makes them attractive?

Here are a few things a bad boy possesses to make your daughter's heart flutter and be attracted to them:

- His charm and talent.

- His genuine popularity (with everyone women and men).

A Father's Rulebook on the Do's and Don'ts for Dating His Little Princess

- ➤ He's full of mystery.
- ➤ He seems strong.
- ➤ Your daughter is tired of being labeled the "good girl".
- ➤ She's eager to uncover and bring out his sweet and lovable side.
- ➤ She ultimately believes that she can change him into her ideal man.

The Breakdown on What a Bad Boy Really Is:

His charm is really his flirting technique, which he has acquired by lots of practice with several girls at the same time.

- ➤ His popularity might be attractive but that only comes from letting every girl know she has a chance with him, even while he's dating another.
- ➤ That mystery comes from him answering all your questions with a simple "Yes," or "No," because he doesn't want to open up or be bothered.
- ➤ Dangerous habits and rages of jealously do not make a man strong. They make him hot-headed and irrational.
- ➤ It's better to be the "good girl" than to be abused by a bad boy. Your daughter can't change him, and he can't change you.
- ➤ Don't enter a relationship trying to bring out someone's "other side." They may not have one? He doesn't show his true emotions for a reason. At the end of the day, it's his way or the highway, no matter how much persuading you do.
- ➤ Your daughter sincerely believes she can change him. No one is! He has to make a choice to figure out his own issues before he can love anyone properly. Besides, your daughter

shouldn't have to fundamentally change someone in order for the relationship to work. He should already meet her most basic standards by the time she views him in a romantic way.

Beware of Wolves Hiding in Sheep's Clothing

A gentleman is not sexist, and neither is he misogynistic. **Misogyny** is the hatred or dislike of women or girls and is not always visible to the untrained eye. Misogyny can be manifested in numerous ways, including sexual discrimination, denigration of women, violence against women, and sexual objectification of women.

The most common form of misogyny from a candidate is sexual objectification of women, teens, and girls and can be misinterpreted as gentlemanly behavior. For comparison, I've listed a gentleman's reason for his actions versus the misogynist's reason for the same action.

From the outside, both actions appear the same, but on the inside, the intent or reason from the misogynist's point-of-view is diametrically opposed to the gentleman's. Below are a few examples of each. Bad versus good!

On opening the door for a lady

Misogynist: "I will open this door for you because you are female, and your limbs are frail, and you haven't built enough muscle to counteract the resistance of the door."

Gentleman: "I'm opening the door for you because I'm a respectable man. As it turns out, I open the door for everyone."

On paying for dinner on the first date

Misogynist: "I'm paying for dinner because I expect something in return...and it starts with the letter 's' and ends with letter 'x.'"

A Father's Rulebook on the Do's and Don'ts for Dating His Little Princess

Gentleman: "I'm paying for dinner because it's courtesy to pay for dinner anytime I invite a guest to join me. This is also why I'm successful in business."

On giving her his jacket when it's cold

Misogynist: "I'll give her my jacket because she forgot to bring one. Always forgetful! Typical woman!"

Gentleman: "She's cold so I will give her my jacket to wear. It's the polite thing to do."

On helping put her luggage in an overhead bin

Misogynist: "She's a woman and doesn't understand men like to pick things up and put things down."

Gentleman: "I will ask her if she would like my help. If she doesn't want it, I'm not offended."

On waiting to sit after she sits

Misogynist: "Why would I wait? Woman, bring me my food!"

Gentleman: "As a host, I wait until any guest has been seated before I sit. It's proper etiquette."

On walking on the outside of the sidewalk (closest to street)

Misogynist: "I walk closest to the street, so I can check out other women driving by."

Gentleman: "I walk closest to the street to protect her from traffic and splashing puddles, and according to feminists, 'There is nothing sexist about cherishing or protecting another person.'"

4 – Sound Dating Advice for the Candidate

Every dating daughter deserves respect and a good dating partner who is upbeat and positive. A candidate never forces his date to do something she doesn't want to do. A date that is planned is often more successful than a date that is thrown together at the last moment. A candidate should date one person exclusively, be faithful and know that trust is the foundation of all relationships. Candidates should ask questions to learn more about the person they're dating. Candidates should never let someone talk him into violating his own principles.

In addition to the straight forward advice above, what most candidates really need are opportunities to develop healthy friendships with girls first, and then see if there's any romantic spark between them. If they kid themselves into believing that a romantic relationship is the "end all to be all" they will undervalue their circle of friends and stop seeing them as importantly as girlfriends. That's wrong! They need to maintain both.

Friendships in the long run are often more meaningful and lasting than romantic relationships. Most of us can relate to this as we're usually more relaxed, open, and trusting with our friends. Why? Because we know and understand each other well enough and the bond between us is strong enough to where we can speak our minds and be ourselves.

So, what's all this leading up to? It's best to start dating a friend and test the waters of teenage dating before diving heart first (not head first) into a romantic relationship. It's safer that way. Romantic relationships are usually based more on physical attraction than common interests. Sometimes it's hard for teenagers in such relationships to admit that and build trust like they would if they started out as friends.

Love Versus Lust

What is love? No one has it completely figured out. I sure don't! If you're daughter isn't sure what it is, she's not alone. That feeling we call love remains magically mysterious because it's different for everyone. Plus, there are many kinds of love: love for a parent, a close relative, a best friend, a sports hero, a mentor, a total stranger in need, and so on.

Then you have the stuff that poets and songwriters have tried to describe for centuries: the ever-intoxicating, pump-up-your-heart-with "joy juice" and "got-to-have-it" romantic love. That's the feeling you get when you think you're with "the one." The one you love may not actually be "the one," but you believe they are until you learn otherwise.

Is it Love?

When your daughter thinks she's found that special someone and she's not sure if it's love or is it simply lust, figuring out the difference can be difficult because intense physical feelings are hard to separate from intense emotions. Love includes feelings of contentment, affection, attraction, and belonging, plus a connection with and concern for each other. Mature adult love may include commitment and a desire to build a lasting partnership and perhaps a family. For candidates, love is often about being with someone they're attracted to and who understands and appreciates them.

Or is it Lust?

Lust, on the other hand, has to do with sexual drive. At this time in a teen's life, their body is buzzing with hormones that come with adolescence. These hormones create strong sexual feelings. Sexual feelings lead to sexual thoughts. The feelings are normal and so are the thoughts associated with them because they're an essential part of human biology.

However, accepting the fact that sexual thoughts and desires are normal doesn't give a candidate the green light to act on them. A teenage boy must learn to control his sexual thoughts through fantasies, writing, music, or art, or better yet, redirecting their sexual energy through sports, exercise, dance, or work. They can also release sexual feelings through masturbation. All of these are safe ways for a teenage boy to lessen their sexual drive and keep them out of trouble.

Why lessen the sexual drive? Because the decision to have sex with someone isn't a simple one. Sex means more than doing something just because it "feels good." It feels good to take a hot shower after you've been out in the cold, or to get a hug from a friend when you're feeling down, or to eat ice cream just about any time. But unlike these activities, the decision to have sex with someone is complicated, and a lot of teens don't understand this until it's too late.

Take the Dad's Truth or Dare Quiz

As a father and parent, you've got to ask yourself this question: Is your daughter dating the testosterone kind of guy you were in your teens? If that question brings back old memories when you were a dating candidate yourself, great. Try to remember what your motive was and what was primarily on your mind back then.

If the answer has you worried, then it's time to take my Dad's Truth or Dare Quiz (located in the Appendix) every father of a dating daughter should take to find out if she's dating the same kind of guy you were in your teens. It's easy, without thinking about the questions below, just answer them as fast and as honestly as possible and see how you score. FYI: There's no right answer.

1. Back when you were a teenage boy, did you think of girls in a sexual way more than ten times a day?

2. If you had the opportunity with no strings attached, would you have sex with a girl, any girl, at least once a day?

3. Does your subconscious automatically interpret non-sexual words into sexual words at least three times a day?

4. When judging a girl, was the first thing you judged her by was her body, or her character?

5. During your summer break in high school, if you were stranded on a tropical island and you had three things to choose from for your own survival, would you pick: A) a 5-gallon container of water? B) a pack of matches to make a fire? or C) the home coming queen naked?

If you answered one of the five questions a "Yes," you're lying to yourself. If you answered two of the five questions "Yes" you're still lying. Three questions? You guessed it, you're lying to yourself! If you answered the first three questions yes, the fourth one "body", and the last one item "C"; you're most likely telling the truth! Truthfully, when I was an adolescent, I would have answered all five questions the same way!

And the truth is always the best. Because once you know truth, you'll know what you're up against and you'll be better able to deal with it. And now that we've established what the norm is, you've got your work cut out for you if you truly want to be a gentleman. So read on!

Building Healthy Relationships

A healthy romantic relationship includes a lot of elements, but here are the basic ones: honesty, respect, trust, communication and the avoidance of jealousy and cheating. If a candidate has the first four ingredients, a relationship can grow in healthy ways. Understanding what a healthy relationship is a key component for any successful dating relationship.

Honesty

Honesty is the freedom for a candidate to be who he really is, without pretending or trying to be somebody else. It means a candidate speaks from the heart and openly shares his feelings and opinions. When a candidate is ready for an honest and open relationship, your daughter never has to wonder if he's telling the truth, because he's always truthful 24 hours a day, seven days a week, and 365 days a year. Without exception!

Some candidates think that lying is acceptable and it solves problems, but it usually creates many more problems than it solves. It's hard covering up lies and as an involved parent, you should be on the lookout for deception, especially when it comes to a candidate's intentions with your daughter's reputation. In the end, lying often causes confusion, guilt, and pain and is never good for any kind of relationship. Period!

Respect

Some people think that they should only respect someone who has a "higher status" than they do. It's true that people in positions of authority often command greater respect. While it's an excellent idea to treat authority figures with respect, real respect has nothing to do with one person being "above" someone else. In fact, in the healthiest relationships, both people feel equal and treat each other respectfully.

To respect someone means you value that person. Maybe you value the person for his or her personality, character traits, or other qualities. Maybe it's because of a certain choice the person has made or the way he or she treats others. When you respect someone, you treat that person in the same way you would like to be treated with kindness, honesty, and consideration.

In relationships that lack respect, one person may feel in control of the other (and may even think that he or she has the "right" to put down, insult, or embarrass the other person). A serious lack of respect in a relationship can lead to verbal, emotional, physical, or sexual abuse. Every daughter must remember they have the right to be treated with the highest respect. It's much better for your daughter to be single than to be in a relationship where she's not being treated with respect.

Trust

Trust means knowing that the candidate has your daughter's well-being in mind. Mutual trust is when your daughter feels the same way. When they both act with honesty and treat each other with respect, they can count on each other. Trust is the foundation of a healthy relationship because it allows both parties to continue to pursue other interests besides dating without incrimination. When you trust someone, and the person is trustworthy, there's no need for jealousy or self-doubt. They're both free to be themselves, which brings out the best in each of them.

Communication

Besides respect and trust, healthy relationships require open communication. That means your daughter and the candidate can talk freely and there are no "off-limit" subjects between them. They're free to express their feelings without judgment. Using open communication, the two of them can learn more about each other on a very personal level and come to understand each other more deeply.

Most problems in romantic relationships result from poor communication, or none at all. It's easy to say you're going to communicate better but doing so is another thing altogether. Many people simply aren't comfortable talking about their feelings, even with family members. To open up may feel a bit strange. However, if your daughter and her date understand how poor communication creates problems, they'll recognize that open communication is an excellent place to start. They should share what they're feeling, even if it seems weird or embarrassing at first.

Jealousy

People in trusting and healthy relationships aren't jealous when their girlfriend or boyfriend spends time with others. In a romantic relationship, often times lovers might express feelings of jealousy if one of them directs their attention towards someone else in a purely innocent or platonic way.

Because of this, they may feel threatened, hurt, confused, angry, and less loved than they were before. It doesn't make a lot of sense when you really think about it, but it happens all the time because feelings get in the way. If your daughter and her date are feeling that way, their relationship most likely lacks trust.

Cheating

The most extreme form of dishonesty in a romantic relationship is cheating on each other. What a candidate and your daughter consider cheating depends on the agreements they've made together. For example, if a candidate agreed not to date anyone else and he does, that's cheating. If your daughter has agreed not to flirt with anyone else and she does, that's cheating. Being dishonest in this way shows a lack of respect for your partner and the relationship as well. And doing something they know is wrong can make them lose respect for each other.

If either person in a romantic relationship is unfaithful to the other, it's going to create problems. So why do people cheat, especially when it can be so hurtful to the person they care about? People cheat for lots of reasons, but mostly because they don't have the maturity or integrity to do the right thing despite what they're feeling, physically and emotionally.

Friends or Something More?

When someone your daughter really like says, "I just want to be friends," it can be hard to take, especially when she sees that person being a romantic interest. She might be hurting, but she's not helpless. She always has choices for handling any situation and should ask herself these questions:

Is a friendship better than nothing? It might be, if you like the person and can put aside your romantic feelings and enjoy the friendship. On the other hand, you may have trouble shelving your emotions. In this case, it may be wiser to choose not to be friends for now.

Can he be a good friend? A candidate may find that he can't be with your daughter without wishing the relationship were more than it is. If so, maybe he can't be a good friend until his romantic feelings subside. In that case, saying "no thanks" is a healthy decision.

Friendships with people that a candidate likes more than "just friends" can work. If, in his heart, the friendship feels right, this could be a great opportunity to learn about himself and what it means to be a true friend. Remember, many successful romantic relationships start out as friendships. This may not happen in his case. But then again, it might!

What is a Gentleman These Days?

Good question and it needs repeating in this chapter. A gentleman is well-mannered and considerate with high standards of proper behavior. That one sentence is paramount to this section and sums up what every dad expects from each and every candidate, without fail, or dereliction of duty.

He's always faithful to what's in the best interest of our daughters and not himself. Another ideal quality of a candidate is to be chivalrous, courteous in behavior, especially towards women.

Taking those concepts one step further, we can see clearly now, that our daughters deserve candidates who are honest, respectful, trustful, believe in open communication and avoid jealousy and cheating.

And they appreciate old fashioned dating habits like the ones below.

Ten Old Fashioned Dating Habits We Should Make Cool Again

I believe in preserving most of the old-fashioned relationships when it comes to teenage dating and think it's important for candidates to take the initiative and ask the girl out because it shows their desire and courage to do so. These are great qualities for dating as well as for everything else in life. If my daughter asks out an acceptable candidate, I'm ok with that because I'm a big proponent of equal opportunity dating.

The experience is new, but the desire is ancient, so no matter how much each generation tries to be different, when you acknowledge the things that really matter, like being a gentleman, faithful and chivalrous, some things never change. Below are ten old fashion dating habits still in style that have stood the test of time that few daughters can resist, and parents admire in a candidate.

1.   *Coming to the door to pick someone up*

In this electronic age of cell phones and texting, don't be surprised if your daughter receives an unromantic "I'm here" text instead of a knock at the door. Of course, meeting someone from online or any circumstance like that would probably be the exception to this rule, but generally the 30 seconds it takes to get out of a car or cab and knock on the door makes a huge difference.

2.   *Trying to dress nicely for a date*

What counts the most with a candidate's attire is not how GQ he looks, but how much effort he put into it to making himself presentable to your daughter. It's not about wearing suits and petticoats again. It's about whether or not a candidate wants to accept the fact that appearance does count for something, and he should do his best to make sure his appearance says something positive about himself and makes a good impression.

3. Bringing flowers or other tokens of affection to the first date

I think there's something that all women will accept without fail, is bringing flowers to her on the first date. You can never be sure how other gifts of affection will be received, but a gesture of flowers confirms a candidate's interest and shows class. I've seen many girls and women reject candy, stuffed animals, and jewelry, but I've never seen one reject flowers (even when they're allergic to them!).

4. Going dancing that's not grinding on a grimy club floor

Whatever happened to sweet and innocent dancing? Dancing for the sake of dancing is fun, not essentially having sex on a dance floor by grinding on it. That's not the way to go. Instead, it's better to get out there and without being obscene and try more subtle moves. Even if you're afraid of dancing, it's better to get out there and try it, then be a wallflower and sit on the bench. The art of slow dancing has generally been lost but is a perfect way to get close to a date, without violating their inner boundaries, if you know what I mean.

5. Straightforwardly asking someone out and not calling it "hanging out"

Today's teens have found convenient ways to skirt around the issue of having to put their hearts on the line and ask (as in talking, not texting) someone out on a date. Asking someone out in person can end up being messy and confusing for all parties involved. But that's ok, they'll get through it. Being direct about whether or not you'd like to go on a date with someone face-to-face is a lost art and one that should be restored.

6. Additionally, being clear about when you're "going steady"

Oh, the awkward, "So… are we… you know… going steady?" talk. Are they hanging out or going steady? Classic question! There's nothing corny about going "old school" and asking one another if they'd like to "go steady." There's something simple and satisfying about asking one another if they'd like to, rather than assuming that they are, or aren't. That can be confusing, so let's be clear about it.

7. *Romantic gestures like writing poems or your own lyrics*

Writing poems may not be for every candidate, and that's understandable, because they're hard to write. But when you think about it, great lyrics from memorable songs, are a form of poetry. Ok, it depends on the lyrics, but you get the point. If you can write lyrics, you can write poetry, or vice a versa. A candidate has other options to express his feelings like a handwritten letter in the mail or just surprising your daughter with something he made even if it looks like the macaroni necklace you made when you were five years old, it's the thought and the time you took to do it that counts.

8. *Turning electronics off and just being with one another*

I'm not sure there is anything worse on a date than the person who picks up their phone and starts staring at it in the middle of dinner, or at any point while you're together and having a conversation. I'm not anti-technology here but I am saying that there comes a time to turn off and disconnect the electronic devices and remember what actually matters most, your date.

9. *The general concept of asking permission for things*

There used to be a principle for people to ask: "Oh, when can I see you? Or, when could I call you?" Versus just assuming they can at any point. I think that old concept could be applied to our modern world by assuming that, unless told otherwise, a candidate should ask your permission to do things with your daughter. Once your daughter is in a relationship, it's still a good habit to keep asking, and not assuming.

10. *Not assuming sex is to be had at any point in time*

I'm certainly not saying that sex should go back to the dark ages and being a taboo subject and an unspoken word around my daughter. But we certainly shouldn't expect it from someone on the third date, the first date, or any date on my watch. A date does not have to be a precursor to sex, and a candidate shouldn't be disappointed if it isn't, because he should never assume that it will be. Get it?

In closing this chapter, I highly recommend that candidate read it backwards and forwards and study it well because there may be a pop quiz on it in Chapter 6: Meeting the Parents and the Candidate Interview.

5 – Setting Boundaries and Establishing the Rules of Engagement

You may think your teenager could care less about what you have to say regarding dating, but current research suggests that parents have a lot more influence than they realize. Not only are they listening, but more importantly, our teenagers are watching their parents closely and modeling their lives after them. Whether you believe it or not, parents are the biggest influence in their teen's life.

Several studies point to a parent's ability to shape their kids in lasting ways, especially during critical milestones like key birthdays, getting their driver's license, and dating their first boyfriend or girlfriend. These rites of passage are important to most teens, and one study revealed that a parent's inactivity or absence during those times made teens more likely to create their own moments by participating in risky behaviors such as drinking, drug use, early sexual activity, and dangerous driving.

The reverse is also true. For teens whose parents were involved during key moments, not only were teens less likely to participate in those same behaviors, but teens were also happier people. Now is the time for you to get into your daughter's dating game and help coach her dating experience so it's a rewarding one that will eventually help prepare her for a lasting and loving relationship and eventually marriage.

Discussing Teen Dating with Your Daughter

Before your daughter goes on her first date, you'll need to set boundaries and establish the rules of engagement for dating. Most of the rules involve common sense, but never assume your daughter and her date possess enough of it. In most cases they won't, and that's where you as a parent can have a big influence with your better judgment, rules, and restrictions come into play.

Every teen is different and so is every dad's and mom's parenting style and skill set. Regardless of what that is, your first objective is to let your daughter know you care about her and her dating experience first and foremost. There're a lot of losers out there, and you're not going to let her date any of them. You just want the best for her and you're there to help make sure that happens.

As a father of a teenage daughter, share with her that you were once like the boys who want to date her. Let her know what you wanted then as a teenage boy, versus what you know now as a grown man, and for those reasons you're very protective of her when it comes to dating. Like any loving parent, you want the best for her.

Starting the Discussion

Depending on who is your daughter's favorite parent at the time, you might want that parent to start the discussion. However, before it's ended, a dad needs to conclude it with what he expects of the candidate for safe and sane dating. This is the one distinct advantage a father has in making your daughter understand what most boys want from a date. Sex!

Yes, it's a fact of life, and there's nothing to be ashamed of. However, the point I'm making is that it's in a young man's genes (as well as his other jeans) to perpetuate our species and plant his seed as far and wide as possible. To be fruitful and multiply is part of our human biology. To have as much sex as possible and with as many females as possible is a young man's basic instinct. This is genetic preprogramming. It's in his DNA. The sooner we accept it, we'll be more prepared for dealing with it.

Dating is a Serious Responsibility

What separates humans from the rest of the animal kingdom? We have a conscious and are aware of our actions, and we know better than to act upon them. There is a time and a place for everything, including sex. But like a young and inexperienced teen who's about to drive a car for the first time on a freeway without ever getting a learner's permit, taking driver education, or passing the driving test, they're going to be a menace on the road and to society and cause a lot of accidents, if not be in a few themselves.

As good parents and citizens, we're not going to let that happen. If our teenagers are going to date, they're going to date responsibly. It's our obligation as parents to make sure that happens and without any rules for engagement and setting boundaries, most of our teenagers, because they're teenagers, will not date responsibly.

With that said, it's a good frame of mind to consider every teenager's hormones and reproductive systems as "armed and dangerous" and "loaded weapons" that are "ready to fire!" Use this chapter as a road map and keep it handy like you would a fire-extinguisher just in case you smell smoke and a fire gets started and is burning.

Matters of Trust

Discussing and setting teen dating rules together with your daughter can be helpful; as it shows her input is valuable. It also helps to establish a mutual agreement from both sides, rather than a dictated set of laws that the teen is expected to follow without a chance for input. It may be helpful to put everything in writing, with parents and teens signing the agreement at the bottom.

Trust is a big factor and it's often up to the teen to prove they're trustworthy, to have responsible friends, and to earn their parent's trust regarding safe and sane dating limits. Sometimes, a rule will start out one way, and after trust is established, the specifics of the rule can be renegotiated. Teens who wish to have any rule changed should talk to their parents about how to build trust and confidence first to earn the changes they would like to make.

Setting Dating Boundaries with Your Daughter

Most teens (and many tweens) become interested in dating at various ages, and parents might need some dating advice to decide which rules are best for them and their family. Adolescents need to know what the rules are, and they most often feel more confident about themselves when clear boundaries and expectations are set. Parents should set limits, for their peace of mind as well as their teen's. Having clearly defined teen dating rules helps parents feel secure knowing where their teens are and who they're with. Rules are a way of bringing structure and predictability to the family, both of which are necessary for maintaining feelings of well-being and trust.

Seven critical dating boundaries need to be covered when it's time to discuss teen dating rules. Whether it means setting the rules together with the teen, or deciding ahead of time what the limits are, these subjects should be discussed well before the first date.

Curfew

What time is the reasonable limit for returning home after a date or evening out? Will the parent be up waiting? Should the teen wake the parent to inform of his or her arrival? Will there be any grace time or flexibility attached to the curfew? What is the procedure if something comes up to prevent the teen from making it home at the appointed time? Discuss these questions and potential outcomes and agree and add any other pieces relevant to your family's needs.

Transportation

Will your daughter be permitted to ride in the car with another teen driving? Often, parents of teens under driving age will not permit their teens to ride with a teen driver, at least without a parent or adult present in the car. Other parents will decide on transportation depending on how long the teen driver has had a driver's license and what their driving record is like, and only after speaking with the driver's parents first. Some parents will allow their teen to go in a car with a group of peers, but not alone with one other teen driving.

Parents of adolescents below driving age, particularly tweens, will probably expect to be chaperoned, either by driving and dropping them off, or making arrangements with the intended date's parents for transportation.

Accompaniment

Get to know all parties involved. Most parents want to meet the person going out with their son or daughter before they allow them to go out with that person. Sometimes, the parents would like to talk with, or even meet the parents of the person their teen wishes to accompany on a date. Parents want to know that the person who will be with their daughter is responsible and will use good judgment and common sense in an unaccompanied situation.

Carry a Cell Phone at All Times

Always carry a cell phone. If you don't want your daughter to have a cell phone, get a prepaid phone that's for emergencies only. Program in her phone your cell number and the number of a trusted friend or relative. Girls should keep their phones in a pocket, not in a purse that can be left behind or stolen. Make sure the phone is charged.

Checking In

Some parents keep in touch with their teens via cell phone (call for emergencies and text for status) or other means while they are away from each other. There may even be a "check in" rule at a specific time to help maintain this trust and having a means of communication can be helpful for this. If your teen plans to go to more than one place, they need to tell their parents when they're leaving the first place and when they expect to be at the second one.

Your daughter needs to call you if she is coming home later than the time she gave you. Making her stay in touch as a habit is a good one so that you know there may be trouble if you don't hear from her or read her text. Seconds and minutes count when you're in a dangerous situation.

Sexual Behavior

Parents should talk with their teen about being responsible, and what kind of intimate behavior is appropriate, according to the moral guidelines in the family. It's important to set up good communication in this subject, as teens are faced with many choices, particularly the ones to have sex or not. A solid foundation of parental expectations will help support your daughter to be candid with you when difficult questions arise.

Teens should always be aware that they have choices and they don't have to do anything that makes them feel uncomfortable. They should also be told by their parents that will always be available to talk if they have questions or concerns regarding dating.

No Drinking and No Drugs

No drinking and no drugs or any kind of illegal substances are permitted. It's a good idea to go over that list to make sure your daughter knows which ones they are. Don't let her date drink or do drugs or any kind of illegal substances either. Never get into a car with someone who is under the influence. If your teen can't find someone sober to take them home, make sure they know they can always call you for this and use their "no questions asked" or "get out of jail card" agreement should they need it.

Emergency Situations

As noted above, many parents have a "no questions asked" or "get out of jail card" agreement should their teen call them to pick them up when they don't feel safe riding with their ride for any reason. Doing the responsible thing and calling parents earns them a "judgment-free" ride home. It also shows them that their safety is the most important priority, and a teen who uses good sense should feel comfortable asking his or her parents for help when it's needed. And when help is not available, your daughter should never be afraid or hesitate to dial "911."

Establishing the Rules of Engagement for Dating

The thought of your daughter going on dates can make even the calmest of parents a little nervous. But it's important to allow your teen the freedom to try dating while she's still living under your roof. Create clear guidelines about your expectations to help your teen understand the importance of healthy relationships and the dangers of sexual activity.

Any rules you choose to create should be dependent upon your child's level of maturity. While some teens can handle group dates before the age of fourteen, others aren't quite mature enough to handle dating until they're older. Here are some rules and guidelines to consider when creating rules for your teen:

Meeting Dad and the Parents

Always insist on meeting your daughter's date. This critical aspect of dating will be discussed in more detail in Chapter 6: Meeting the Parents and the Candidate Interview. Ask to meet your date's parents as well if you have the opportunity. Since most teens are a reflection of their parents, you can sometimes learn more about the candidate by learning more about their parents.

Get to Know Anyone Your Teen Wants to Date

Make sure you get to know anyone your teen is going on a date with. If a boy pulls up and honks the horn from the driveway instead of coming in to meet you, make it clear that your daughter isn't going on a date with him. You can always start by meeting a date at your home a few times for dinner before allowing your teen to go out on a date alone.

Know Who, What, Where and When

Make sure you have a clear itinerary for your teen's date. For younger teens, inviting a romantic interest to the house may be the extent of dating that is necessary. Or you can drive them to the movies or a public place. But older teens are likely to want to go out on dates on their own without you. Make it clear you need to know the details of who your teen will be with, where they are going, and who will be there with them.

Date in Groups and Around Responsible People Preferred

Stay around other people on a date. Parking in the middle of nowhere or going to a house where nobody is home are both invitations to sexual pressure or dangerous encounters with strangers. If you're around other people, you'll have safety in numbers and you'll hopefully have a friend nearby who can talk you out of dangerous decisions.

No Dating Older People

Each state has laws about dating older people. In some states, teens can date anyone they want once they reach sixteen, but in other states they don't have that choice until they turn eighteen. Legal issues aside, parents should set the rules about dating older people. There's usually a big difference in maturity level between a fourteen and an eighteen-year-old. There may be more pressure to have sex or a fourteen-year-old may struggle to be assertive with an older date. Encourage your teen to date people who are closer to their age.

Keep the Bedroom Door Open

If your daughter invites a date into your home, make a rule that says the door must stay open. Teens that are given complete privacy are likely to grow tempted to engage in sexual activity. Establish clear expectations about the importance of having conversation and doing activities together that don't involve sexual activity.

Know Who is Home at the Other Person's House

If your teen is going to a date's home, find out who will be home with them. Have a conversation with the date's parents to talk about their rules. Other families may not have any set rules or may not see the need to provide any type of supervision, or their rules are different than yours. So, it's important to inquire in a polite but straightforward manner what type of rules and supervision will be offered.

Discuss Technology Dangers

Technology can be problematic for teens involved in romantic relationships in several ways. With the advent of the internet, Tweets, Facebook, and camera phones, inappropriate photos and texts can become public and unsuspecting teens can have their reputations ruined with the "click" of the "send" command.

Soliciting and passing along photos of underage teens on your phone or computer that contain nudity (known as sexting) can also have legal consequences. If a boy receives a photo of his girlfriend in various stages of undress, or the other way around, and he passes it along to his friends, he could receive charges for distributing child pornography. It's essential that parents discuss the dangers of sharing sexual conversations and photos through the internet. It's a serious topic!

Other Dad's Tough Rules for Dating Their Daughter!

By now, you should be fired up and ready to handle your daughter's first date. If so, you're on the right track and to help make sure you don't get too fired up and out of control, I've included for your reading pleasure a hilarious blog from Gunz (reposted by Gawfer) about the perils of dating his teenage daughter through his eyes.

It's titled "Ten Simple Rules for Dating My Daughter" and it's an internet classic that went viral in 2006 that borrowed the key elements from Bruce W. Cameron's book; *Eight Simple Rules for Dating My Teenage Daughter: And Other Tips from a Beleaguered Father*. It would be an injustice if I didn't quote him word for word and include Gunz's iconic photo in this chapter (actually Marlon Brando's photo from the movie "Apocalypse Now").

Please note the ten rules are his spin on dating his daughter for any candidate brave enough to do so and don't necessarily reflect the

A Father's Rulebook on the Do's and Don'ts for Dating His Little Princess

views of the author. However, in a twisted yet funny way, his message appeals on a gut level most every father of a dating teenage daughter and is presented solely to entertain you and not be followed as gospel.

So, if your daughter thinks you're being too harsh or restrictive with her and her date, just have her read these rules below and let her know you're not that bad, at least compared to this dad, but could be if you had to. Enjoy!

Ten Simple Rules for Dating My Daughter

Posted by Gunz on his Freedom, GUNZ, Glory, and Ebyjo blog on Sept. 1, 2006

So You Want to Date My Daughter?

""Wanna date my daughter, heh?

Speak the perimeter password, announce in a clear voice that you have brought my daughter home safely and early, then return to your car - there is no need for you to come inside. The camouflaged face at the window is mine."

Rule One: If you pull into my driveway and honk you'd better be delivering a package, because you're sure not picking anything up.

Rule Two: You do not touch my daughter in front of me. You may glance at her, so long as you do not peer at anything below her neck. If you cannot keep your eyes or hands off of my daughter's body, I will remove them.

Rule Three: I am aware that it is considered fashionable for boys of your age to wear their trousers so loosely that they appear to be falling off their hips. Please don't take this as an insult, but you and all of your friends are complete idiots. Still, I want to be fair and open minded about this issue, so I propose his compromise: You may come to the door with your underwear showing and your pants ten sizes too big, and I will not object. However, in order to ensure that your clothes do not, in fact, come off during the course of your date with my daughter, I will take my electric nail gun and fasten your trousers securely in place to your waist.

Rule Four: I'm sure you've been told that in today's world, sex without utilizing a "barrier method" of some kind can kill you. Let me elaborate, when it comes to sex, I am the barrier, and I will kill you.

Rule Five: It is usually understood that in order for us to get to know each other, we should talk about sports, politics, and other issues of the day. Please do not do this. The only information I require from you is an indication of when you expect to have my daughter safely back at my house, and the only word I need from you on this subject is "early."

A Father's Rulebook on the Do's and Don'ts for Dating His Little Princess

Rule Six: I have no doubt you are a popular fellow, with many opportunities to date other girls. This is fine with me as long as it is okay with my daughter. Otherwise, once you have gone out with my little girl, you will continue to date no one but her until she is finished with you. If you make her cry, I will make you cry.

Rule Seven: As you stand in my front hallway, waiting for my daughter to appear, and more than an hour goes by, do not sigh and fidget. If you want to be on time for the movie, you should not be dating. My daughter is putting on her makeup, a process that can take longer than painting the Golden Gate Bridge. Instead of just standing there, why don't you do something useful, like changing the oil in my truck?

Rule Eight: The following places are not appropriate for a date with my daughter: Places where there are beds, sofas, or anything softer than a wooden stool. Places where there are no parents, policemen, or nuns within eyesight. Places where there is darkness. Places where there is dancing, holding hands, or happiness. Places where the ambient temperature is warm enough to induce my daughter to wear shorts, tank tops, midriff T-shirts, or anything other than overalls, a sweater, and a goose down parka-zipped up to her throat. Movies with a strong romantic or sexual theme are to be avoided; movies which feature chain saws are okay. Football games are okay. Old folk's homes are better.

Rule Nine: Do not lie to me. On issues relating to my daughter, I am the all-knowing, merciless god of your universe. If I ask you where you are going and with whom, you have one chance to tell me the truth, the whole truth and nothing but the truth. I have a shotgun, a shovel, and five acres behind the house. Do not trifle with me.

Rule Ten: Be afraid. Be very afraid. It takes very little for me to mistake the sound of your car in the driveway for a chopper coming in over a rice paddy in Vietnam. When my PTSD starts acting up, the voices in my head frequently tell me to clean the guns as I wait for you to bring my daughter home. As soon as you pull into the driveway you should exit your car with both hands in plain sight. Speak the perimeter password, announce in a clear voice that you have brought my daughter home safely and early, and then return to your car; there is no need for you to come inside. The camouflaged face at the window is mine.

As a father, I hope it also relieved some tension and anxiety about your daughter coming of age and dating. You're going to need all the amusement and relief you can get, because now comes the next step with meeting the candidate and interviewing him before he goes on his first date with your daughter.

6 – Meeting the Parents and the Candidate Interview

There are many horror stories to go around about first-time meetings with parents, and movies like "Meet the Parents" are a comical reminder of what can go wrong. It can be a nerve-racking experience. That's why it's essential for the candidate to be prepared and take the meeting seriously.

The interview is crucial and can be done ahead of the date departure time, preferably in your living room, dining room or kitchen. You can also meet with the candidate even earlier if that works best with your schedule at a place of your choosing. It really doesn't matter where you meet, but that you meet, so that when the interview is over, you're comfortable enough to allow this candidate to date your daughter (or not date her).

Meeting the Candidate

Upon meeting the candidate in person, this is your best opportunity to ask him all the questions that concern you and get to know him before you lay down the rules of dating your daughter. How you do this is up to you. But just do it! If you don't, you might end up kicking yourself in your butt after a bad date, because you didn't make a big enough presence at the interview. You have the advantage of being the "all-knowing and all-powerful" dad. Use it!

If the candidate has never dated a girl that has an interview process like this one, he must be feeling more nervous than usual, now that you have him on the defensive. This is a great time to let the candidate know that you took these measures to meet with him because your little princess is extra special, and you only want the best for your little girl. You could even go on and ask him if he were a father, wouldn't he do the same for his daughter? Of course, he would, and once the candidate buys into this, your daughter's dating experience can only be better for it.

Upon your first impression of the candidate, should you judge a book by its cover or not, so to speak? The answer to this is yes and no! If he comes to the interview with baggy pants and they're sagging as well, I would immediately inform him that they're not acceptable and that he comes back at a later time when they are up to his waist like they should be. If he's not tall or handsome or the color or religion you were expecting, you're going to have to look past these superficial characteristics and look deeper into the content of his character which is what really matters. Don't start thinking what your grandkids are going to look like because odds are against this candidate being the one she'll marry and have kids with.

Starting the Interview

If you're unsure how to start the interview and what to ask the candidate, don't sweat it as I've prepared a helpful outline for you to follow. You can modify the interview outline as you see best, use what you need, and ignore the rest. There's no wrong or right way to use the outline. It's just there to give some good questions to ask and a script to follow if you need one.

I must warn you though that some of the questions are brutally honest, some are comical, some are straight forward, some are over-the-top, and some are trick questions. The main purpose of the outline is to start a dialogue between the parent(s) and the candidate by asking easy, neutral, and tough questions as needed to elicit the candidate's true intentions, values, and personality.

A Father's Rulebook on the Do's and Don'ts for Dating His Little Princess

Every candidate is different! Every interview is different! Every date is different! If you feel that you need to error on the side of tough questions, that's alright, because your daughter means everything to you and any gentleman being interviewed for the first time would understand that his date's dad only wants the best for her and he will settle for nothing less. And you should too, because every daughter deserves a gentleman.

Name, Address, City, Zip Code, Home Phone, Cell Number, E-mail Address and Age

Besides asking the candidate the typical info above, be sure to get his age as well. A general rule is a candidate should be in the same grade as my daughter and not more than one year older. If she's in elementary school, don't allow a middle (intermediate or junior high) school candidate to date her, nor allow a middle or junior high school daughter to date a candidate in high school. And when she gets to high school, don't allow her to date a candidate that's in college.

Nickname

Most nicknames are harmless, unless you're in a gang or a player, so depending on the nickname, the next question to ask is how did he earn it? Or is it something he made up to impress people, or your daughter? The answer could reveal a lot about his personality!

Do You Have Social Media Type Postings?

If the candidate has any social media postings, ask your daughter if he's invited her as a friend and if you can check out his account. If she's embarrassed about his account and its content, then he's not the right date for her.

School, Grade, and GPA

If his GPA is less than 2.5 he's less than average and if you're like any self-respecting dad, you want the best for your daughter, and will not accept any GPA less than 3.0. If your daughter is honor roll and highly academic I would raise the minimum GPA to date my daughter to a level that is commensurate with her academic standing and your expectations. All high school sports require a minimum GPA to play, or sit on the bench, so why shouldn't dating be any different?

How Many Times a Month Do You and Your Family Attend <u>Any</u> Kind of Worship or Religious Service?

I'm not preaching religion here as I'm a longstanding Agnostic. However, there is overwhelming data that clearly indicates religious beliefs and practices (most any kind) are associated with higher levels of marital happiness and stability, stronger parent-child relationships, and greater educational aspirations and attainment, to name a few of the benefits. Of course, you don't have to attend in any kind of religious activity or with any frequency to be a good person or a desirable candidate, but it doesn't hurt.

Do You Do Community Service?

Community service is a great litmus test for a candidate, provided it was voluntary and it wasn't assigned to him for being on probation. Does he perform volunteer work, is a teacher's aide, do mentoring, tutoring, or help out in any way possible? These are all good questions to ask if the previous question's answer wasn't the one you were expecting.

Do Your Teachers Generally Like You? List Any Academic and Citizenship Award, and What Do You Plan on Doing After You Graduate High School?

A teacher student relationship is a good indicator of how he deals with authority figures. Academic and citizenship awards speak for themselves. What the candidate plans on doing after he graduates high school is a good indicator of where he's headed in life.

How Many Times Have You Visited the Principal's Office for Disciplinary Action? Have You Ever Been Suspended or Expelled from School?

If you haven't already caught on by now, and I bet you have, the application form is laced with trick, trip-you-up, or game over type of questions. Any disciplinary actions that show up on these questions, unless they have a very good reason, are deal breakers.

Do You Have Two Parents? Are They Divorced?

Information about the parents is very important as candidates from a stable household with two parents will "usually but not always" have more positive outcomes such as being less likely to engage in pre-marital sex and get someone pregnant.

Were You Raised by a Single Parent? How Old Was Your Mom When She Got Pregnant with You?

On the opposite extreme, candidates who were raised by one parent, particularly a teenage parent, will most likely have more negative outcomes such as a higher likelihood to engage in pre-marital sex and get someone pregnant.

What are Your Favorite Hobbies, Sports, Talents, Pastimes, and Things to Do? What is Your Favorite Movie and/or Video Game?

It's good to know what these are to see if they match your daughter's likes and even yours. A favorite movie or video game will reveal if the candidate has an overtly violent side, likes fast cars and women, and is preparing for Armageddon.

Do You Have a Part Time Job?

Having a part time job is a good thing, as long as it's not as a male stripper.

Do You Have a Driver's License? Or Learner's Permit? If Yes to Either, Please Provide the Number

If there's any doubt about whether or not your daughter will be safe with the candidate behind the wheel of his car during a date, you might want to inspect and/or check his license and driving record to make sure he's a safe and responsible driver.

How Many Traffic Tickets Have You Received? For What Kind of Ticket? Do You Own a Car? What Kind? Is it Insured?

If the candidate has a part time job, that's a plus. If he has a driver's license and you want to check his driving record, ask him to provide his license number in case you feel inclined to check with your local DMV to see how many traffic tickets he's received and for what kind of violation. Car insurance is a must.

Does Your Ride Have Pimp Rims and Excessive Sound System? Does Your Ride Have Tinted Windows? Does Your Ride Scrape the Bottom of the Driveway if You Don't Slow Down?

If the candidate owns his vehicle, it's good to know if it has pimp rims and excessive sound system as this may be the first warning signs of the hip-hop gangsta lifestyle, not to mention a public nuisance (the music part, not the rims part).

If you can't see into the candidate windows, neither will the police if something is happening inside that is against the law. This could be another sign of the hip-hop gangsta lifestyle, not to mention that annoying feeling that they can see you, but you can't see them inside their car.

If the candidate's vehicle is so low that it scrapes the bottom of most driveway approaches unless it slows to a crawl, this could be another potential sign of the hip-hop gangsta lifestyle, not to mention the scrape marks on your driveway.

List the Three Most Important Things About My Daughter That Appeals to You.

If the candidate lists tits and ass as two of his three most important things he likes about your daughter, you can be sure he's only after one thing. If he lists her face, or eyes, or nose, and things like a laugh, a giggle, a smile, he's looking deeper than T & A. If he goes on to list personality traits about her that you know them to be true, he's on the right track.

Which of These Three Words Would Sum Up What Kind of Relationship You Expect with My Daughter?

If the candidate picks a "Friend," like all dads, I'm ok with that. However, if he turns out to be gay or bi-sexual and he's using my daughter as a cover, or he's not sure himself, he's wasting her time and he can "find himself" elsewhere. If he chooses "Boyfriend" which is what I'm expecting, certain conditions apply as noted above. If he notes "Lover" I'm thinking he's going all the way and that's not the kind of candidate I'm going to allow to date my daughter.

Do You Have Another Girlfriend at the Present Time? Are You Ok with Dating More Than Two Girls at the Same Time?

Two more trick questions and if the answer is yes to either one, he's a player and he can go play somewhere else but not on my shift with my daughter's heart and aspirations.

Do You Wear Baggy Pants? If Yes, How Low Do They Go? State the Lowness Here in Inches.

Under no circumstances whatsoever will I allow my daughter to date a candidate with saggin' baggy trousers. This is my biggest personal taboo! There is no excuse for this type of gangsta' attire which has been outlawed in many school districts, cities, and states as indecent exposure. It's too bad we can't hand out tickets as well for poor taste.

Where Do You Typically Hang Out At?

If he's hanging out with his posse, at an arcade, the mall, the liquor store, the racetrack, the projects, etc. he's not going to be the right fit for your daughter. If his other hangouts are not where he can apply his studies or improve his character, I'd be suspicious if he's going to be the kind of candidate you want your daughter to be with.

If Your Peers Were to Categorize You in Your Yearbook, Would They Categorize You as a (Fill in the Blank)

Look deep into what the candidate writes candidly about himself and if you come across the words "Player" or "Lover" or "Gangsta'", need I say more? You know the answer: He's not right for your daughter, or any daughter.

What Are Your Three Favorite Rap Artists?

Another trick questions because having one modern rap artist would disqualify the candidate. Why you ask? It's very simple: Any music and lyrics that promote cop killing, drug running, and pimping life styles will not be tolerated and anyone proud enough to admit that has the wrong set of values for my daughter. FYI, when Rap first came out decades ago, it wasn't like that.

Are You a Good Freak Dancer?

That kind of dancing was acceptable amongst adults in the movie "Dirty Dancing," but not with my daughter. With my daughter's reputation at stake, I would not allow anyone to grind on her at a dance in any way or from.

Do You Believe in Pre-Marital Sex?

You're thinking it! Would any candidate be dumb enough to answer "Yes" to this one? He better not, if he wants any chance of dating my daughter.

A Father's Rulebook on the Do's and Don'ts for Dating His Little Princess

Are You Familiar with the Statutory Rape Law?

Another trick question that begs another question if he answered "Yes." How would know about such things?

Do You Have Any Distinguishing Tattoos?

I'm not a fan of tattoos for the simple reason: Why would inject ink into your skin of an image that you wouldn't feel proud about hanging as a painting on your living room wall? If it's a sport, ROTC, or club tattoo that the candidate is passionate about, I can understand that and accept it.

Would You Describe Yourself as a Non-Drinker, Casual Drinker, or Heavy Drinker?

Because minors cannot consume alcoholic beverages, the candidate's answer better be the first one. Any other answer is grounds for dismissal because most teens are not responsible drinkers.

Do You Smoke?

For the same reasons as the previous question, minors cannot smoke cigarettes. Although smoking cigarettes is not a criminal offense if you're a minor (and that age may vary from state to state) selling them to a minor is.

Please Check Each of the Illegal Drugs You've Taken

If a candidate has checked any of them, he'll never get the chance to date my daughter, and must have been high when he responded!

Do You Have a Criminal Record? Belong to a Gang?

Need I explain this one? If so, the candidate's answers should be "No! and "No way!"

What Makes You Special Enough to Date My Daughter?

Here is the extra credit question that offers some level of redemption to undo some of the candidate's poor answer choices. Furthermore, no one is perfect, and I certainly wasn't at that age, so if at least the candidate was honest with his answers, some or all of the wrong answers can be forgiven here. However, the level of redemption all depends on the answer and how many questions the candidate answered wrong to begin with. It's your call dad!

Concluding the Interview

If you're satisfied at the end of the interview that candidate's likes and dislikes match your daughters and that he appears to be a gentleman, the two of them are good to go on a date. If you have some reservations about the trustworthiness of the candidate from his answers, make them known, and see how he responds to them. If you're satisfied or reasonably satisfied, let them go on the date, and state any qualifications for the date and make sure both your daughter and the candidate agree to them.

However, if the candidate doesn't make the grade and you have some serious concerns about him dating your daughter, how do you handle this delicate situation? Every parent will handle this differently, but the best advice I can give is to pay close attention to the candidate's likes and dislikes and see if they match your daughters. If they don't share common interests, I doubt there is any basis for the relationship to begin with, so this could be the basis for not approving the date vs. personally criticizing the candidate's answers and your daughter's choice of him.

If he almost makes the grade, you might want to give him one chance to date your daughter to see how it goes. If your daughter is set on the date and ignores your advice, as a dad and a parent, it's your right to deny permission and work out another option, perhaps as a chaperone, or a home date, under close supervision. For some great tips on chaperoning and when it's appropriate, visit Chapter 17: Chaperoning Proms, Parties and Driving.

A Father's Rulebook on the Do's and Don'ts for Dating His Little Princess

Application Form for Permission to Date My Daughter

On a lighter note to help dads relax even more and prepare their questions for the candidate interview, you can download my Application Form for Permission to Date My Daughter which covers all of the above questions as a pdf document or a Word document so that you can modify it yourself with your own questions and make your own copy. To do this, please check out the Appendix for more instructions.

One word of caution using the form: Use it as a last resort if you have serious doubts about the candidate. Use it during the interview or develop your own or modify it and ask only those questions you or your daughter feel comfortable with. Be flexible!

I showed the form to my daughter ahead of her date and she hated the idea of me asking those questions on an interview or having her date fill it out so we made an agreement between us: I would never subject her date to those kind of questions on an interview or have him complete the form ahead of time, if she promised to make sure that her date would not flunk the interview and instead "ace" it and make me proud. She agreed and so did I!

The goal of the application form is to put parents at ease with humor from some of the tough questions and also show them there is a very serious side to some of them as well. The main purpose is to start the dialogue and get parents thinking about what are the best qualities for a candidate, if he and your daughter are going to be compatible, and if he's going to be a gentleman.

Why take any chances with your daughter's well-being? There's too much at stake when it comes to tween and teen aged dating, so never be intimidated about asking tough, direct, and trick questions to dig deep for the truth. You have the right as a parent and also because you care deeply about your daughter's well-being. Don't be afraid to use it as needed.

7 – A Single Parent's Playbook

Parents may be single due to separation, divorce, or death, or they may have never been married. Also, some parents may have a partner who is not able to help with parenting due to a disability or a job that takes them away from their family most of the time.

Besides a great resource for single parent's, this chapter is also a handy reference for the married spouse filling in for the other, or a step parent, stepping into a new role. This happens frequently when either is serving our country overseas, travels a lot, works long hours, or an absentee parent which in most cases, but not all, is the father.

Parents in different situations face different challenges, but in all of these cases, it is hard enough raising teenagers with two parents, let alone one. Being a single parent can be hard on teenagers, who often wish they could have more of their parents' attention and may have emotional issues to work through, because there may be only one parent available at any given time, instead of two. The most important way to deal with these handicaps is through direct and unrestricted communication with your child.

Couples splitting up is never a pretty sight. Neither party leaves without emotional scars. However, the biggest victims and perhaps the most hurt by this split are the children. Stuck in a situation that they have no control over and suffering consequences for something that had no role in, kids are challenged at an emotional level that may even test the nerves and patience of a strong adult. Forced into a single parent family, kids become vulnerable to various psychological effects, some of which can be disastrous for their dating years as an adolescent.

If you recall from the previous chapter, there were two very important questions about the candidate's parents, asking if they had two parents or were raised by a single parent. As the statistics below will show, there are more positive outcomes of having two parents than a single one.

Do You Have Two Parents? Are They Divorced?

Information about the parents is very important as candidates from a stable household with two parents will "usually but not always" have more desirable outcomes. "Like what?" you may ask. Consider the following. Candidates with two parents who are not divorced will most likely:

- Have a higher GPA than a candidate raised or living with a single parent.
- Have a greater chance to go to college.
- Have no criminal record.
- Have a lesser likelihood of engaging in pre-marital sex.
- Have a lesser chance of getting your daughter pregnant.
- Have a lesser likelihood of sexually abusing your daughter.
- Have a lesser chance of contacting and spreading STD's.

Were You Raised by a Single Parent? How Old Was Your Mom When She Got Pregnant with You?

On the opposite extreme, candidates who were raised by one parent, particularly a teenage parent, had more negative outcomes, and were most likely to:

- Have a lower GPA than a candidate raised or living with two parents.
- Have a lesser chance to go to college.
- Have a criminal record.
- Have a greater likelihood of engaging in pre-marital sex.
- Have a higher risk of getting your daughter pregnant.
- Have a greater likelihood of sexually abusing your daughter.
- Have a greater chance of contacting and spreading STD's.

As far as what age the candidate's mom gave birth to him, this may be a difficult question to ask, but considering there are so many teenager mothers out there (i.e., children having children), I would ask it.

Resentment and Sense of Inferiority

Kids want both their parents to be there with them and for them to feel whole, but when the split happens, they are reduced to just one parent and their self-worth may be diminished. Single parents can try their very best to not let their kids feel the absence of the missing parent. But that is usually impossible, and by themselves, they just can't fill the void. Kids hear their peers talking about how good their parents are and get reminded of their own circumstances, which they might resent.

This resentment leads to feelings of inferiority, which in turn may affect their overall confidence. They stop believing in themselves and just want to be left alone. They have trouble making friends, talking to people, and setting goals for themselves. This feeling of inferiority increases overtime and has negative psychosocial effects that can ruin their chances for a healthy relationship for life. As a single parent, nothing makes as much difference as building a strong relationship with your teen to overcome these handicaps.

Our outlook on life can be significantly defined by our experiences. These events, changes or developments can have a much more powerful influence if they occur during childhood. Children of single parents can develop negative beliefs and attitudes about relationships. The divorce, separation or death of a parent can be too stressful for a teen. Single parents need to help their kids accept and adapt to the situation, enabling them to foster healthy relationships in future.

The teen might lose trust in the institution of marriage altogether. The divorce and the post-divorce conflict might cause aversion to the idea of marriage or a long-term commitment. They might never want to tie the knot, because in their mind, untying that knot is what caused their family so much stress.

They might prefer to tie flimsy threads instead. This could lead to frivolous love affairs or risky sexual behavior. It could deprive them from the contentment of a strong relationship based on trust and respect.

How Can You Minimize the Damage?

Do not let teens suffer the consequences of something they're not responsible for. Single parents raising children have the huge responsibility of treating teens cautiously and considerately through the transition. You should not let the episode take its toll on your kid's future relationships.

Have age appropriate conversations with your kids. Explain to them the reason for the separation or the divorce. Let them know how strong relationships take work and time, and how they are built upon trust. Do not make the episode appear as a devastating event or the norm. Emphasize how it is natural for relationships not to work at times. Parting ways is not meant to create problems, but to solve them. Back up your words with actions.

Even if it's hard for you to accept the death of your spouse or get over a painful break-up, try not to have a sullen countenance for a long time. The sooner you normalize things, the better it is for your child or teen.

In case of a divorce, try to model co-operative behavior with your spouse. If kids see you treating each other with respect, they might not think of the break-up as the end of their lives. Continuing to receive love from both the parents and seeing them respect each other's opinions could prevent the teen from post break-up trauma.

A smooth transition will prevent your teen from adopting a negative approach to future relationships. The teen would deduce the magnitude of the event from your reaction to it. In case of a break-up, it is essential to teach them about relationship-building for the future. Explain the parting of ways in a way that does not make them dread commitment or think of it as a substitute for working things out.

The transition, if it wasn't made smoothly, could also lead to extreme all-or-nothing attitudes. Kids may later on adopt the habit of quitting relationships in case of a conflict. They might consider ending things as the easy way out. On the other hand, some might become totally submissive. Their low self-esteem could make them accept disrespectful behavior from their partner.

Additional Measures and Support

Don't be afraid to seek outside support. While the parent is busy making ends meet and working full time, grandparents or close relatives and friends can give a helping hand in taking care of the kids in their absence. Support groups like Online Parent Support and others can help single parents feel encouraged. Family and friends can also help and being involved in community or church groups can relieve loneliness for single parents and give adolescents positive role models. If your parenting system isn't working due to financial pressures, then the community and government can step in and help out to make the situation better for the family.

In most cases, a single parent will be a single mom. If that's your situation, resist saying negative things about the absent father. This may be very hard, but it's not good for teenagers to hear their mothers say bad things about their fathers, which may lead to feelings of anger and resentment. This doesn't mean the mother should "make up" good things, but they should refrain from saying bad things. An absentee father at first, may end up being more present in the future. As the expression goes, "better late, then never!"

Emotional Pressures of Single Parenting on Teens

In a major study conducted by Swedish researchers on single parenting, it was revealed that children from single parent families are twice as vulnerable to mental health issues, substance abuse problem and attempted suicide. An estimated 41% of children are born outside the marriage with single parents. According to the latest survey carried out by the U.S. Census Bureau, approximately 28% of the children in the U.S. are living in single parent families.

Dr. Keith Ablow, a psychiatrist has outlined several psychological effects of single parenting on children. He believes that, single parenting issues, if not treated properly, can bear serious consequences on the lives of children.

The most important thing at play in a single parent home is poverty. Census 2012 revealed that 24% of single parent families are ones with single moms; of which 80% live in poverty. This narrows down the opportunities for kids and develops low self-esteem among them, including a lot of other issues.

Time is a casualty in single parent families. Single parents are rarely available for their kids because they have bills to pay, work to do, places to be at, etc. From sunrise to sun down, the single parent has to do all the chores at home and manage work along with it. This leaves them with very little time to spend with their kids. Lack of their parent's attention makes the teens feel depressed and unwanted; and in order to fill that void, they, often, seek company which may be harmful for them. And that could also apply to whom they date. Kids are always hungry for love and attention. Fulfilling that need can be challenging with two parents, let alone a single parent.

Single Parents by the Numbers

According to Custodial Mothers and Fathers and Their Child Support: 2009, a report released by the U.S. Census Bureau every two years (and most recently in December 2011), there are approximately 13.7 million single parents in the United States today, and those parents are responsible for raising 22 million children. This number represents approximately 26% of children under twenty-on in the U.S. today. Ouch!

Despite negative assumptions that most single moms "selfishly" chose to raise their kids solo, the majority of individuals raising children alone started out in committed relationships and never expected to be single parents. The presumption that most single parents are mothers is accurate. According to the Census data:

- Approximately 82.2% of custodial parents are mothers.
- 17.8% of custodial parents (approximately 1 in 6) are fathers.

The assumption that "most" single mothers are single from the outset is false. Of the mothers who are custodial parents:

- 44.2% are currently divorced or separated.
- 36.8% have never been married.
- 18% are married (and in most cases, these numbers represent women who have remarried).

- 1.1% were widowed.

Of the fathers who are custodial parents:

- 53.5% are divorced or separated.
- 24.7% have never married.

The Challenges of Single Parenting in America

The single parent statistics shown below bring to light some of the challenges of single parenting in America.

- 23% of teens live with only a mother, four percent live with only a father, and four percent live with neither parent.
- Three percent live with unmarried parents.
- About 40% of teenagers were born to unmarried mothers.
- Black teenagers are the most likely to be raised by a single mother, followed by Hispanic, then white teenagers, with Asians the least.
- Teenagers living with only one parent have financial and educational disadvantages compared to teenagers with both parents, especially if their parent is the mother and if she did not finish high school.
- Slightly more than one in four teenagers in America are being raised by a single mother.

Number of Single Parents Continues to Rise

According to the latest single parent statistics, are we experiencing an epidemic of single parenting in the U.S.? Yes!

Single parenting is not a new phenomenon. In fact, the number of single parents raising children in the U.S. has been on the rise for decades. According to the latest single parent statistics reported in the article Unmarried and Single Americans Week Sept. 18-24, 2011:

> 11.7 million single parents were living with their children in 2010.

> 9.9 million of those single parents were custodial single moms.

> 1.8 million of those single parents were custodial single dads.

According to these figures, approximately 85% of single parent households are headed by custodial single moms, while fifteen percent are headed by custodial single dads.

According to the latest single parent statistics (and some of them don't match exactly prior or later notations, but nonetheless are close and drive the point home), how many children are being raised in single parent households compared to two-parent households? According to America's Families and Living Arrangements: 2010:

> 69.4% of American children live with both parents.

> 23.1% of American children live with their mother only.

> 3.4% of American children live with their father only.

> 4.1% of American children live with neither parent.

In addition, according to Single Parent Households by Country:

> 19.5% of households with children were headed by a single parent in 1980.

> 29.5% of American households with children were headed by a single parent in 2008.

Obviously, rising divorce rates contribute to the increase in single parent households. According to the latest single parent statistics, are more unmarried women choosing to have children today than ever before? In a report Births to Unmarried Women by Country, the answer is yes.

- ➢ 18.4% of all births in the U.S. in 1980 were to unmarried women.
- ➢ 40.6% of all births in the U.S. in 2008 were to unmarried women.

These are horrifying statistics, further amplified by comparison to the lower unmarried birth rates in the 1970s, 1960s and 1950s.

Conclusion: Avoid Being a Single Parent if Possible

Take extra precautions with a dating candidate from a single-parent household. Like every statistic noted throughout this book, the figures are merely averages, and every individual, should be evaluated on an individual basis, and not a statistic. It all comes down to content of character and character counts above all other traits. Every person is unique and every situation different. Respect that!

Nonetheless, the overwhelming negative statistics of raising teens by a single parent are very conclusive and speak for themselves, and it's up to each and every parent to use them as they see best. As one of two sons of a single mother, I can speak for myself personally to the many handicaps she endured raising two strong willed boys on her own and to the handicaps my brother and I had ourselves without the positive effects of a father figure and a two-parent household.

Some Personal Facts and Lessons

On the negative side, I experienced six expulsions and three trips to juvenile hall during my teen years, raised by a single mom, and was clearly not a well-adjusted teenage boy and certainly not an ideal candidate for dating. On the positive side, my mom raised me to be a gentleman and treat women with respect like the way she wanted to be treated. Regardless of the questions, I could ask her anything (and I mean anything) about sex and she would answer me first hand without sugar coating it. In that regard, armed with good advice, I wore protection and never got anyone pregnant, nor did I catch an STD or abuse my dates. Thanks mom!

My younger brother Todd, had even more issues than I had. He never fully matured in character as a responsible adult male, got a dear friend of ours pregnant, was incarcerated more times than I can remember, and engaged in unprotected sex which eventually led him to contacting the HIV virus, and succumbing to AIDS. There is no doubt in my mind to this day, had we both been brought up in a stable two parent family, he would still be alive today and I would have been a more acceptable candidate.

As a father of a teenage daughter, would I be comfortable with her dating someone like me when I was her age? The answer would still be no. The reasons why are because I had room for improvement in being more emotionally mature and engaging in healthy relationships as well as becoming a true gentleman.

It wasn't until I joined a fraternity that I learned how to be a mature young man and a true gentleman. To help me perfect being a true gentleman, I had the good fortune of being taught the gentlemanly arts by the greatest "gentleman master" I have ever known: Dave von Fleckles, who is also the actor playing the father in the "So You Want to Date My Daughter?" video.

8 – Parenting Styles and Dating Forms

For many decades, researchers have witnessed various parenting styles being adopted by parents across the globe for nurturing a healthy relationship with their children. What parenting style they opt for their children is significant as its effects remain with the children as they grow up into teens and then adults.

Different types of parenting styles have different effects on teens. From how developed your teens daily routine is, to how they behave in public and private, to how they feel about themselves; all of these aspects are a result of a certain parenting style you have adopted and shown them. Therefore, it's vital to ensure your parenting style is providing healthy relationships and adolescent development to your children.

The Four Styles of Parenting

Below is a brief overview of the four different types of parenting styles. It's good to see what they are so you know what your style is. Starting at the top of the list, the authoritative parent is the ideal type, and the other three; authoritarian, permissive and neglectful, are more and more less desirable as you work your way down the list.

Each style defines what sort of a role parents have in their teen's life. If you begin to see yourself as falling into one of the last three categories, you might want to consider changing your style to fit the needs of your daughter and what's best for the two of you in your parent child relationship.

On the lighter side, if you need some role models to choose from, or not to choose from, I've include a list of TV's most popular dads for your review and enjoyment at the end of this chapter. Have fun with the list!

Getting back to the serious side of things, let's find out more about these parenting styles in detail below and which one you currently fall into.

Authoritative Parenting

This type of parenting style has proved to be most healthy and beneficial for teen's growth and development. Authoritative parents create clear rules for their teens and also allow for reasonable exceptions to those rules. They use logical consequences to teach their teens life lessons. Moreover, they also adopt a positive discipline at home to reinforce good behavior among their teens and also prevent them from adopting certain behavioral problems.

This is usually done by creating a system that rewards their good behavior. In case teens do something wrong, parents take them in their confidence and make them realize their mistakes in order to prevent them from not committing the same mistake in future.

Teens raised with an authoritative parenting style tend to be content and successful in the long run. They become good decision makers and can evaluate safety risks on their own. In short, children who have authoritative parents tend to become responsible adults who feel confident and do not waver while expressing their opinions.

Authoritarian Parenting

Unlike authoritative parents, authoritarian (...ive vs. ...ian word endings) parents believe teens should follow the rules without being given any exceptions. Without regarding their teen's opinions, they create and enforce rules on them. As a result, these teens miss out on getting involved in any problem-solving challenges.

Authoritarian parents only want to enforce their rules on their teens and expect unquestioned obedience from them in return. Instead of teaching discipline, such parents only punish their children to teach them a lesson. Children may follow rules while growing up with strict parents, but they may also develop self-respect problems. They may become aggressive when they grow up or are likely to become good liars to avoid any kind of punishment. This type of parenting style can be harmful to the teen's growth and development.

Permissive Parenting

As the name suggests, permissive parents are quite lenient. They may set rules but rarely enforce them on their children. They only step in when teens are going through a serious problem. Otherwise, they remain negligent. When children do something, they rarely give out any consequences, hence there is no reward or punishment system. Even if permissive parents do react, they usually give in too quickly when their child promises or begs to be good in future.

Basically, they're quite forgiving and friendly and allow kids to do whatever they may want. Children raised with a permissive parenting style start taking their parents as their friends. Parents encourage them to talk with them about their problems and life struggles but do not put much effort into dispiriting their bad choices. As a result, their bad behaviors are also not discouraged entirely.

Growing up with such parents can be problematic for the teens as they not only struggle academically but also adopt behavioral problems. They may also be prone to developing health problems such as obesity, physical dormancy, and dental cavities because permissive parents find it difficult to control their junk food intake.

Neglectful Parenting

Also, often termed as uninvolved parenting, this type of parenting style is notorious for being the most harmful for the children. Basically, neglectful parents tend to be negligent towards their child's growth and development and expect them to raise themselves without offering any help from their end. They rarely devote any time or energy into meeting their kid's basic or social needs.

While some parents are neglectful towards their children deliberately, there are also uninvolved parents who happen to be like that unintentionally. For instance, a parent with some mental health issues or any other serious health related problem may not be able to look after a child's physical or emotional needs consistently. Neglectful parents lack information about their child's education, their social life, and even their whereabouts.

At times they're so engrossed in their own busy work schedules that they pay no heed towards their child's development. In such cases, children may be subject to inferiority complex as they do not receive much parental attention. They struggle with self-esteem problems and perform poorly in academics. Neglectful parenting style can create behavioral problems in teens and make them unhappy and depressed.

The Four Basic Teenager Character Types

Just as personalities vary from one adult to another, personalities in teens vary as well. But teens do share some personality characteristics because they share a common biological state that releases large amounts of life-changing hormones during their adolescent years. Parents of teens should expect and prepare to accommodate these common teen personality characteristics.

Learning what these common teen personality characteristics are beforehand can help with preparing your approach to teen dating and what level of management and intervention is required by the parent and what level of supervision and instruction is needed by the teenager. Of course, teens are more complex than these four categories, but by reviewing each one, you might discover what characteristics are driving your teen's behavior.

Independent

When your teen was younger, getting along with him was probably easier. The teen years make life hard on parents because of a teen's need to become independent. This desire for independence is an evolutionary one, teens are maturing and preparing themselves to enter the adult world.

They understand they cannot rely on their parents forever. The result is a teen who is more autonomous and emphasizes their own ability to make decisions and their right to privacy. In this respect, parents will usually find their teen's goals diverging from their own.

Risk Seeking

Although the amount of risk-seeking varies in teens, few demographic groups exceed teens in terms of risk-seeking activities. The reason for this lies in the teen brain. Dr. Paul Martiquet, medical health officer and author of the article "The Teenage Brain," notes that the brain of a teenager is not fully developed, especially in the frontal lobes.

Because the frontal lobes of a brain are the primary source of decision-making and consequence-evaluation, teens tend to be weak in understanding the connection between their actions and the possible negative outcomes. Thus, even risk-averse teens will occasionally act in ways that seem foolish in their parents' eyes. For example, while young, a tattoo might seem cool, but teens often neglect the fact that a tattoo lasts a lifetime (unless you go through the removal process).

Extraverted

Even introverted children become more extraverted in their teen years. While this does not mean an introverted teen becomes a socialite, it does mean she will begin to focus on making friends and gaining a social standing in her peer group.

The teenage years are a training period for adulthood, a time in which relationships are crucial in getting along in the world. Parents should expect children entering their teens to want to spend more time with their friends than with their families. Even at home, teens might feel compelled to get on the computer to use social media platforms rather than talk with mom and dad.

Romantic

Perhaps "romantic" is not the best word to describe inexperienced teenagers, but they are often prone to describe themselves this way. Romantic or not, one new aspect of the teenage years is the flood of hormones flowing through their bodies that pushes them to engage in romantic encounters.

For some teens this results in harmless flirting, but for others it results in early sex, which has its own consequences. Nevertheless, parents cannot control a child's biology and thus must use education as a way of helping their teens avoid or protect themselves from the risks that their hormones push them to seek out.

In general, if your daughter falls into any one of the four categories, you might want to consider some additional means and measures to ensure safe and sane dating. To help in that regard I've included a copy of the following forms at the end of this section for consideration.

- Application Form for Permission to Date My Daughter
- Permission to Date My Daughter Contract and Agreement Form

The "Application" and "Permission" to Date My Daughter Forms

"An application form! Are you serious? No freaking way!" I heard my daughter say the first time I mentioned them. It's the one thing she despised the most, more than anything else was the Application Form for Permission to Date My Daughter and even more so the Permission to Date My Daughter Contract and Agreement Form.

When it comes to my daughter's well-being, I'm dead serious about using the form if I have too. And besides, after reading Gunz's hilarious rules of engagement (a dad's alter ego), an application form is relatively harmless. What better way to show how serious a candidate is about dating your daughter and for you to show how you serious you take it, than to require each new candidate to fill out a form and to insist upon it?

You can find more information in the Appendix on how to access both forms.

Application Form for Permission to Date My Daughter

There is a lot that can be learned about a candidate from the questions on the Application Form for Permission to Date My Daughter already covered in this chapter. The questions on the form are one of the most effective screening devices as well. True, you can't know everything about the candidate from a form, but it can reveal many undesirable characteristics that may be cause for concern and help you screen a less than desirable candidate from dating your daughter.

Permission to Date My Daughter Contract and Agreement Form

Upon successfully completing the application form and interview process and then receiving your permission to date your daughter, the next step is for the candidate to read, review, and sign the extra copy of the Permission to Date My Daughter Contract and Agreement Form and make a copy if possible of the form for you, her and the candidate. Signed, sealed, and delivered!

Not Using Any of the Forms

As noted earlier, my daughter hates the forms with a passion! She's read every part of them and insists she'll never subject her date something so impersonal as filling out a form to date her. "It's too humiliating to my date!" she'd say. As contentious as this sounds, just the threat of using the form has had the desired effect, because she knows that if the candidate doesn't meet the high standards on it and flunks it, so to speak, he's not worthy of her and she knows that is the intent of the form, and no date for him.

My daughter at the time was (and still is) exceptionally bright and precocious for her age, and this I had to take into consideration based on our daddy-daughter relationship and the whole dating process. I trusted her to not lower her standards, and she trusted me to have faith in her dating choices.

So, she never needed the forms. In fact, her mom insisted the most stringent requirement for dating our daughter was for the candidate to have a GPA as high or higher than hers. And because she continually ranked in the top ten of her class, that requirement alone eliminated all but a small handful of candidates. Good job mom!

If your daughter feels the same way as mine did, and you think you can get by without the forms, don't make the candidate fill one out. However, I do recommend using them as an outline, scaled down or modified to your own personal preferences and/or for the candidate's interview.

If you're uncomfortable with this process and using the forms, don't be ashamed if you are. To help give you some extra inspiration, you may need a role model to come across just the way you want to, feared, respected, and to the point.

Favorite TV Dad's (Most With Daughters) Personas

If you're a bit unsure of your parenting style as a dad and how you may come across to the candidate, look no further to one of your favorite TV dads for inspiration. I'm serious about this! Well, almost.

If you're scoffing at the idea, consider that most sitcoms and TV shows portray real life situations (in a funny and dramatic way of course), but the real issues dealing with right and wrong behavior does have a moral message, regardless of the era they debuted in and watched.

When you find a dad's approach to these issues that you admire and are comfortable with, put your "game face" on and use it. If you're

A Father's Rulebook on the Do's and Don'ts for Dating His Little Princess

unsure of which one works best for you, here is a list of the most popular TV dads (with dating daughters) of all time.

On the other hand, some of listed TV dads I would stay clear of unless it's your intent to freak out the candidate, make him think you're going to cause him bodily harm or leave a lasting impression on him that he'll never forget.

- *Al Bundy (Married with Children)*
- *Alex Stone (The Donna Reed Show)*
- *Andy Brown (Everwood)*
- *Andy Sipowicz (NYPD Blue)*
- *Andy Taylor (The Andy Griffith Show)*
- *Archie Bunker (All in the Family)*
- *Ben Cartwright (Bonanza)*
- *Ben Wyatt (Parks and Recreation)*
- *Benjamin Sisko (Star Trek: Deep Space Nine)*
- *Bernie Mac (Bernie Mac)*
- *Carl Winslow (Family Matters)*
- *Charles Ingalls (Little House on the Prairie)*
- *Chester A. Riley (Life of Riley)*
- *Cliff Huxtable (The Cosby Show)*
- *Dan Conner (Roseanne)*
- *Danny Williams (Make Room for Daddy)*
- *Doug Lawrence (Family)*

So You Want to Date My Daughter?

- Eric Camden (7th Heaven)
- Eric Taylor (Friday Night Lights)
- Forrest Bedford (I'll Fly Away)
- Frank Constanza (Seinfeld)
- Fred Sanford (Sanford and Son)
- George Jefferson (The Jeffersons)
- George Lopez (The George Lopez Show)
- Gomez Addams (The Addams Family)
- Graham Chase (My So-Called Life)
- Herman Munster (The Munsters)
- Homer Simpson (The Simpsons)
- Howard Cunningham (Happy Days)
- Jack Bauer (24 Hours)
- Jack Bristow (Alias)
- James Evans, Sr. (Full House)
- Jason Seaver (Growing Pains)
- Jim Anderson (Father Knows Best)
- Jim Walsh (Beverly Hills, 90210)
- John Robinson (Lost in Space)
- John Walton, Sr. (The Waltons)
- Lucas McCain (The Rifleman)

A Father's Rulebook on the Do's and Don'ts for Dating His Little Princess

- *Marshall Eriksen (How I Met Your Mother)*
- *Martin Crane (Frasier)*
- *Martin Lane (The Patty Duke Show)*
- *Michael Kyle (My Wife and Kids)*
- *Michael Steadman (Thirtysomething)*
- *Mike Brady (The Brady Bunch)*
- *Mr. Sheffield (The Nanny)*
- *Ozzie Nelson (The Adventures of Ozzie & Harriet)*
- *Paul Hennessy (8 Simple Rules)*
- *Phil Dunphy (Modern Family)*
- *Philip Banks (The Fresh Prince of Bel-Air)*
- *Ray Barone (Everybody Loves Raymond)*
- *Red Foreman (That 70's Show)*
- *Rick Sammler (once and Again)*
- *Rob Petrie (The Dick Van Dyke Show)*
- *Rocky Rockford (The Rockford Files)*
- *Sandy Cohen (The OC)*
- *Steve Douglas (My Three Sons)*
- *Steven Keaton (Family Ties)*
- *Tim Taylor (Home Improvement)*
- *Tom Bradford (Eight is Enough)*

So You Want to Date My Daughter?

- *Tom Corbett (Courtship of Eddie's Father)*
- *Tony Micelli (Who's the Boss?)*
- *Ward Cleaver (Leave it to Beaver)*
- *Will Girardi (Joan of Arcadia)*

A Father's Rulebook on the Do's and Don'ts for Dating His Little Princess

Application Form for Permission to Date My Daughter

Name:_____ Age:_____
Address:_____
City: _____ Zip Code: _____
Home Phone #: _____Cell #_____
E-mail Address:_____ Nickname:_____
Do you have any Facebook and Twitter accounts and You Tube postings? Yes___ No___
School:_____ Grade:_____ GPA:_____
How many times a month does you and your family attend <u>any</u> kind of worship or religious service? _____
Do you do community service? Yes___ No___
Do your teachers generally like you? Yes_____ Maybe_____ No way_____
List any academic and citizenship awards:
_____
What do you plan on doing after you graduate high school?
_____
How many times have you visited the principal's office for disciplinary action?_____
Have you ever been suspended or expelled from school? Yes___ No_____
Do you have two parents? Yes___ No___ Are they divorced? Yes___ No___
Were you raised by a single parent? Yes___ No___ How old was your mom when she got pregnant with you? _____
What are your favorite hobbies, sports, talents, pastimes, and things to do:
_____
What is your favorite movie and/or video game:
_____
Do you have a part time job? Yes___ No___
Do you have a driver's license? Yes___ No___ Or learner's permit? Yes____ No___ If yes to either, please provide the number:_____
How many traffic tickets have you received? ___ For what kind of ticket?_____
Do you own a car? Yes___ No___ If yes, what kind?_____
Is it insured? Yes___ No___
Does your ride have pimp rims? Yes___ No___
Does your ride have an excessive sound system? Yes___ No___

So You Want to Date My Daughter?

Does your ride have tinted windows? Yes___ No___
Does your ride scrape bottom of your driveway if you don't slow down? Yes___ No___
What does abstinence mean to you?_____
What is the first thing you notice about a girl?_____
What is the going rate for a motel?_____
List the three most important things about my daughter that appeal to you:
1. _____
2. _____
3. _____
Which of these three items would sum up what kind of relationship you expect with my daughter? Friend_____ Boyfriend_____ Lover_____
Do you have another girlfriend at the present time? Yes___ No___
Are you ok with dating more than two girls at the same time? Yes___ No___
Do you wear baggy pants? Yes___ No___ If yes, how low do they go? State the lowness here in inches: _____
Where to you typically hang out at?_____
If your peers were to categorize you in your yearbook, would they categorize you as a (fill in the blank):_____
What are your three favorite Rap or Hip-Hop artists?
1st: _____
2nd: _____
3rd: _____
Do you believe in pre-marital sex? Yes___ No___
Are you familiar with the statutory rape law? Yes___ No___
Do you have any distinguishing tattoos or body piercings? Yes___ No___
Would you describe yourself as a non-drinker, casual drinker, or heavy drinker? Non_____ Casual_____ Heavy_____
Do you smoke? Yes___ No___
Please check each of the illegal drugs you've taken: Marijuana___ Cocaine___ Mushrooms___ LSD___ Meth___ Other___
Do you have a criminal record? Yes___ No___
Belong to a gang? Yes___ No___ Maybe___ Undecided___
What makes you special enough to date my daughter (in your own words below)?

A Father's Rulebook on the Do's and Don'ts for Dating His Little Princess

_____
_____
_____
_____
_____
_____
_____
_____
_____
_____

So You Want to Date My Daughter?

Permission to Date My Daughter Contract and Agreement Form

I, (print name) _____, do solemnly swear upon my most sacred oath, that I shall respect and honor _____ and treat her like a lady and princess and behave like a gentleman at all times, according to all the rules and requirements expected of me by her father, my date, and the rules of common decency, and under no circumstance, shall I deviate from these requirements and principles and disrespect her in any way or form, or ruin her reputation, or make her cry.

Upon receiving my date from her dad, I shall always provide her father with the time I expect to return his daughter safely home, where we are going for our date, and make sure prior to the date, that my cell phone is fully charged and that it will receive a signal so that my date's father can call and check up on me and his daughter to see how things are going.

Upon any deviation or violation of these dating privileges, they will be immediately revoked, and this contract shall be null and void, and I shall cease and desist from any further contact with my date without her father's express permission. I fully accept these requirements on my own good will and to prove my sincerity, I will sign and date this contract and agreement form below.

_____   _____
Candidate's Signature   Date

_____   _____
Father's Signature   Date

9 – The Art of Dating

Have you ever noticed that certain people, no matter what they look like, always seem to get positive attention? Why is that? Probably because of their self-confidence. They smile, make eye contact, act friendly, and are genuinely interested in others. This makes other people feel comfortable around them. Great advice for both daughter and candidate and parents in the know when it comes to teenage dating.

If you lack self-confidence and the fear of asking someone out is preventing you from dating, what have you got to lose to make that happen? This chapter is a beginner's guide to take that first step. If you let fear keep you from getting to know someone you like, you'll be left wondering "What if?" But if you make the effort to reach out to other people, all kinds of wonderful things might happen.

Asking Someone Out

Dating offers no guarantees, but you can take steps to make the asking out process a little easier. It can be scary to ask someone for a date, no doubt about that. Obviously, you want the person to say yes, but what if they don't? Here are a few tips that may help you get through it:

➤ The answer's no? Fine, you're one step closer to a yes.

- Will your feelings be hurt? Probably a little.
- Will you survive? Absolutely!

Keep one thing in mind, and you'll get over the disappointment much faster if you move on after a "no." Don't waste time longing for people who don't want to be in a relationship with you. The best boyfriends and girlfriends are the ones who like you as much as you like them. Forget about the rest.

Ask Someone You Know

It's less stressful to ask out someone you know, rather than a stranger. If you ask someone you don't know to go out with you, the odds of getting a yes are less than if you ask a person who already knows and likes you. Also, if you don't know the person you're going out on a date with, you might quickly discover you don't really have much in common or enjoy spending time together. Then you're on a date that can feel awkward and very long.

Get Friendly with the Person First

There's nothing wrong with being attracted to someone you don't know, but just because the person you like is "hot" doesn't automatically mean that he or she would make a fun date or a great boyfriend or girlfriend. Take the time to get to know a person before you ask him or her out. This gives the other person a chance to get to know and feel comfortable with you, too.

Once the two of you become friendly, or even close friends, you can decide whether you're interested in moving into the boyfriend or girlfriend zone. Remember, people who know and like each other as friends first stand a better chance of having a healthy and romantic relationship than people who don't know each other at all.

Take a Deep Breath and Go for It

Suppose you've found the courage to start a conversation with someone you like, and the two of you have become friends. Maybe now you like this person even more than before. What's your next move? You can ask him or her out.

You can never win if you're not willing to play the game. Dating can be fun and stressful at the same time and a learning experience either way. It's a great opportunity to get out in the world and discover what's important to you in a relationship. So, take the plunge and ask the big question, "Will you go out with me?"

What Does Going Out Mean to You?

Before you do this, be clear in your mind about what "going out" means. People in various parts of the country have different words to describe phases of dating and relationships, but the explanations are essentially the same. Depending on where you live, asking someone to "go out" could mean:

> ➤ You like each other, and you may or may not be willing to let other people know it.

> ➤ You hang out together, at lunch and in between classes, exchange notes, talk to each other on the phone, and send email.

> ➤ You go places together, as a couple within a larger group of friends.

> ➤ Or, you go places as a couple, just the two of you, also called "dating." Some teens may "go out with" (or "go with") someone for only a few days, or hours, before the relationship ends.

Asking the person you like out on a real date involves more of an emotional risk. Planning the date is part of getting to know each other better, and the date itself is a way to find out whether you enjoy spending time together outside of school.

In the planning stages, you must decide whether to go to a movie or some other place, and get parental permission first, as covered in Chapter 6: Meeting the Parents and the Candidate Interview. You also need to decide on transportation and who pays for what. In other words, going on a real date takes more planning than simply writing notes or hanging out at school.

Going on a date with someone doesn't necessarily mean you're in a romantic relationship. Lots of people go on one date and choose not to go out together again, for whatever reason. To confuse matters, just because you're dating someone doesn't necessarily mean you cannot also be dating other people. The important thing to remember is to keep the lines of communication open. Without making agreements about the relationship (for example, is it all right to see other people?), misunderstandings happen, and feelings get hurt.

When You Have an Agreement

When two people have an agreement that neither of them will date anyone else, it's considered to be an exclusive relationship. In this type of relationship, the couple might go out on dates or just spend time together.

Again, the ground rules for flirting or being sexual with someone outside of the relationship must be agreed upon ahead of time, so there's no confusion. If you're not ready for a serious relationship, consider dating casually, which means going on dates with people you're interested in, but not committing to an exclusive relationship yet.

Before we consider the best practices between dating teens, let's first focus on some thoughtful suggestions for the parents first. My advice is for the candidate to do some research about his date's parents, the dad in particular, and focus on these essential tips, and the do's and don'ts for the first time he dates their daughter.

Timing

It's all about the timing when you meet the parents. Discuss what it means to your partner, for some people, meeting their parents is no big deal, and for others it's huge. Either way, you should assess how serious you are in the relationship because no matter how your partner feels, his or her parents will notice whether you're sincere or not.

Prepare

Prepare for your visit! Ask your partner questions about his or her parents. Getting some background information will help to make conversation. Also, find out who you'll be meeting, and what to call them. It could be awkward if you're trying to make conversation and you don't know what to call your date's mom, "Mrs. Smith" or "Mary?" If there are any special customs that the parents follow, be sure to ask questions about those, too.

Punctuality

Please be punctual! First impressions are lasting, and you want to make a good one. If you're going to be late, it better be for a good reason, then be sure to have a fully charged mobile phone and their number to make them aware of that ahead of time.

Bear Gifts

Even if your date's parents say no gifts, try to bring one anyway. There's always something small and appropriate that can be gifted, your research will pay off here. A bottle of wine is always appropriate for a dinner meeting but typically unattainable for a minor. If the family doesn't drink, or if you're meeting for lunch or something more casual, chocolates, specialty coffee or flowers are appropriate. If nothing else, bring a great smile.

Dress to Impress

This should be a no-brainer, but next to being punctual, proper grooming is essential for a good first impression. Do research on where you're meeting, and what the parents are like. Are they super casual? For guys, nice jeans or slacks with a proper shirt and blazer is appropriate, and you can alter those depending on where you're meeting. For women, no short skirts or cleavage-bearing tops. Or are they very formal?

The rule of thumb here is to dress more conservatively than you usually would while still being yourself. Your date should know what his or her parents expect and can guide you here. If your girlfriend tells you to put on a full suit, just shut up and do it.

Politeness

Another no-brainer, be polite to your partner's parents! After dinner, ask if you can chip in with cleanup or dishes or take the trash out. Be sure to say "please" and "thank you" often. Guys, put the toilet seat down, ladies, sit with your legs closed. What matters most of all is how you treat your partner's parents, family members, and even family pets and property, as it will reflect on how you treat their son or daughter.

Conversation

Again, research is important here! You'll be able to make relevant, engaging conversation if you know a little about your partner's parents. Topics to avoid: Religion, politics, race, and sex are a few of the touchy topics that can ruin a meeting.

If you're going to talk about any of these things, be sure that you're not the one that starts it. All parents are different, some are more open or strict than others, so just feel the situation out, look for clues, and react accordingly.

A topic of conversation that always goes over well is about their son and your daughter. Your daughter should portray her date in a positive light, and maybe share a great story about him. If she can't, maybe he's not worth dating?

What Makes a Good Boyfriend or Girlfriend?

Suppose you have all the close friends you need at the moment, but a part of you is still looking for a boyfriend or girlfriend. If you're searching for the "perfect" guy or girl, it's time for a reality check. No matter how great someone looks, sounds, and acts, no one is perfect. Movies, television, magazines, and romance novels may lead you to believe otherwise, but it's all just hype.

A Father's Rulebook on the Do's and Don'ts for Dating His Little Princess

Here's the truth: There may be someone who's right for you, but this person may not at all resemble your mental image of your dream guy or girl. That's why it's important to determine what you're really looking for in a relationship beneath the surface. What makes someone a good match for you? To increase your chances of recognizing the right person when you meet, you have to know what you really want and need.

To find out what's important to you, create a "What Matters Most" list. It will help you sort out what you want in a boyfriend or girlfriend. Don't focus too much on appearance when you're making this list. Instead, think about personal qualities or strengths you admire in people.

Once you have a clearer image of the characteristics you're looking for, it's easier to recognize a potential match. Plus, you'll be more likely to avoid relationships that have little chance of working out.

What Girls Like in a Date

Some of the more popular things girls like on a date or in a relationship are guys who:

- Adore them. This is the number one thing for girls. Many a girl has fallen in love with a guy after he announces that he likes her. The more you like her, the better (unless it is overbearing).

- Are strong in presence, not necessarily in size. They like guys who are confident and give them the feeling that they are safe when they are around them.

- Aren't afraid to say sweet things to them. "You look lovely tonight." Stuff like that.

- Don't shy away from them when their buddies are around.

- Know how to have fun when they are with a girl (besides being physical).

- Make them feel special. Girls like guys who care about their feelings and who aren't afraid to talk about "emotional" stuff.

- Are thoughtful, who call just to say "hi," "good night," or to see how they are doing.

- Are generous. Not just with money but in other ways, too. They like guys who will go out of their way to make them feel comfortable.

- Take care of themselves. They like clean hair, nice clothes, and they love a guy who smells good.

- Do little thing like hold their hand softly, move their hair away from their face for them, or remember the day they first kissed.

What Guys Like in a Date

Some of the more popular things guys like on a date or in a relationship are girls who:

- Take good care of themselves. This isn't about model beauty. This is about clean hair, smelling good, exercising. By taking care of yourself, you send out the message that you care about yourself. Guys like this!

- Have a life. They like it when you aren't always available. They like to know that if they like you, you aren't going to be needing them all the time.

- Have a sense of humor. This is one of the most underestimated attributes. Let's face it, we all love someone makes us laugh (or laugh at their jokes) and knows how to have fun.

- Don't try too hard. Once again, the message you send when you try too hard is that you are desperate. They want to think that they lucked out by getting you.

- Listen to them and find them interesting. Don't fake it, but don't try to "get" a guy if you don't think he is interesting.

- Have fun with their own girlfriends. They want to know that if they are going to watch the game on Saturday night, you aren't going to fall apart. They like girls who can have a good time without them.

- Sincerely like them. So, instead of thinking, "I want a boyfriend," think, "I am looking forward to meeting a guy I like who likes me back."

Ten Best Gentleman and Dating Movies with Lessons Learned

The dating experience may be new, but the desire to do so is not. No matter how much each generation tries to be different, when you acknowledge the things that really matter, like being a gentleman, acting chivalrous when appropriate, and always possessing the seven pillars of character, some things never change.

Even though times have changed, if my daughter asks out an acceptable candidate, as I mentioned before, I'm ok with that because I'm also a big proponent of equal opportunity dating. Still, I'm a strong believer in preserving most of the old-fashioned relationships when it comes to teenage dating. Why? It's important for candidates to take the initiative and ask the girl out because it shows their desire and courage to do so.

To help with seeing those qualities and to laugh and learn from these romantic and comedic engagements, below are my top ten favorite romance movies that in some way or form demonstrate gentlemanly behavior, chivalry and character, against all odds. Take note candidates and daughters with the character transformations from the beginning of the move to the end, and if there is anything along the way to be learned from them to help you with the art of dating.

"The Princess Bride"

This romantic comedy is a about a make-believe fairy tale with the story centering on Buttercup, a farm girl who has been chosen as the princess bride to Prince Humperdinck of Florian. Buttercup does not love him (he's an older guy!) and still laments the death of her one true love, Westley, a hired hand her age on her farm. Westley went away to sea only to be killed by the Dread Pirate Roberts (not really, that's the rumor she's told as to why he never returns for her, so she gives up on her "true love"). However, Westley returns from the sea alive and well as a swashbuckling pirate and gentlemen to save his Buttercup from the arranged marriage, armed bandits, and the Prince's attempt to have his henchmen kill Westley at all costs, before he can rescue his one true love Buttercup and stop the marriage before the wedding vows are taken. Another good lesson on never giving up on your true love and doing as the daughter wishes.

"Romancing the Stone"

Joan Wilder is a successful author of romance novels and the complete opposite of Angelina, the heroine in her novels. Angelina is a strong, confident woman who is swept off her feet by the stories' hero, a man named Jessie. Joan, on the other hand, is afraid of life and never takes chances. However, when her sister Elaine is kidnapped and ransomed in Columbia and she has to travel there herself to save her with the ransom, she is swept off her feet (literally) after being rescued by an American con artist there, named Jack, a real-life Jessie (sort of), who transforms himself from a selfish treasure hunter to a loving and deserving gentleman, and saves Joan and her sister from the kidnapper's evil plans for them. Complete transformation of Jack.

"My Big Fat Greek Wedding"

Toula Portokalos is 30, from an immigrant Greek family, and works in her family's restaurant in Chicago. All her father Gus wants is for her to get married to a nice Greek boy (she's homely at first but with some TLC, her inner beauty shines through and she turns into a swan), but Toula is looking for more in life. Her mother convinces

Gus to let her take some computer classes at college, so she can take over her aunt's travel agency where she meets Ian Miller, a high school English teacher (a WASP). They date secretly for a while before her father finds out and is livid over her dating a non-Greek. Good movie for dads accepting candidates that may not look like what they were expecting from their daughter.

"High School Musical"

Troy Bolton and Gabriella Montez are at a ski resort during winter break where they are forced to sing karaoke together but afterwards exchange numbers and back at high school become friends quickly and decide to audition for the Winter Musical in pairs. Troy is a popular basketball player and Gabriella is a girl Einstein. They get callbacks, and social cliques they belong to don't approve of this new friendship and try to separate them led by Chad and Taylor, as well as the drama queen Sharpay Evans and her brother Ryan. Gentlemanly and ladylike (as well as catchy tunes) behavior help win the audition for the musical pair of Troy and Gabriella, and the lesson of this movie (besides opposites attract), is to not let your close friends interfere with your dating relationships.

"Hitch"

Alex Hitchens, better known as Hitch, is New York City's greatest matchmaker. Love is his job and he'll get you the girl of your dreams in just three easy dates (guaranteed!). And that's exactly what happens when Albert Brenneman, a chubby accountant, who wins the heart of a gorgeous society heiress Allegra Cole. So, when tabloid columnist Sarah Melas decides to uncover the secret behind Albert's success, she's shocked to discover that Alex Hitchens, the charming young man she's been seeing, is the legendary date doctor himself. Exposed in a front-page story, it's now up to Alex to try to save Albert and Allegra's friendship as well as his own with Sarah. The lesson here is when you think you've found true love, there's always a hitch.

"Roman Holiday"

Princess Anne embarks on a tour of European capitals with her royal entourage, and while in Rome, begins to rebel against her restricted, regimented schedule. On her first night there, Anne sneaks out of her room in disguise, to escape her palatial confinement, and explore the streets of Rome on her own. But the Princess is lost and is found asleep on a public bench by Joe Bradley, an American newspaper reporter stationed in Rome. Concerned, Joe takes her back to his apartment where she sleeps on his bed and he on the couch before he dashes off later that morning to cover the Princess Anne press conference. When Princess Anne doesn't show, he realizes she is the young woman sleeping on his couch and he has the story of a lifetime! However, if the truth gets out, it will ruin Anne's good name and royal standing, so as a gentleman, he passes on the story to save her reputation.

"Jerry Maguire"

Jerry Maguire is a successful sports agent, and has it all, until one night he questions his purpose, his place in the world, and finally comes to terms with what's wrong with his career and life (he's not meeting the seven pillars of character). Recording all his thoughts in a mission statement he shares at work, Jerry has a new lease on life. Unfortunately, his opinions aren't met with enthusiasm from his superiors and after dishonorably being stripped of his high earning clients and elite status within the agency, Jerry leaves the firm to start his own sports business armed with only one volatile client (Rod Tidwell) and his faithful administrative assistant, a single mom (Dorothy Boyd) who believes in his abilities and mission statement. After hitting bottom, Jerry finds true love in Dorothy, because she completes him as a couple.

"Roxanne"

Charlie is a fire chief in a small town in Washington where Roxanne rents a house for the summer to look at comets. Charlie is intelligent, funny, and sensitive, but all his fine qualities are overshadowed by his very large nose. Charlie's new fireman, Chris, on the other hand, is quite attractive, but superficial and awkward with words, especially around women. Seeing no chance at winning Roxanne's heart, the fire chief coaches Chris using Charlie's words to woe her. Unknown to Roxanne, her discourse with Chris is Charlie's words and thoughts (and not Chris'), and she falls in love with the poetry and touching words coming from Chris' mouth, leaving Charlie sad and lonely when Roxanne reveals she would love any man who spoke those words, regardless of his looks. Moral: Inner beauty conquers exterior package and Charlie ends up getting the girl for those reasons.

"Sleepless in Seattle"

After his wife Maggie passes away, Sam Baldwin and his eight-year-old son Jonah relocate from Chicago to Seattle to escape the grief associated with Maggie's death. Eighteen months later Sam is still grieving and can't sleep, so on Christmas Eve, Sam (on Jonah's initiative) ends up pouring his heart out on a national radio talk show about his magical and perfect marriage to Maggie, and how much he still misses her. Among the many women who hear Sam's story and fall in love with him (over the radio) because of it, is Annie Reed, a Baltimore based newspaper writer. Annie's infatuation with Sam's story moves her to write to Sam proposing they meet atop the Empire State Building on Valentine's Day to see if it's true. Is there a second chance at love in Sam's life? Watch the move and find out (and don't give up on your own on second chances).

"Meet the Parents"

Greg Focker is a male nurse, who is ready to propose to his girlfriend Pam. However, he discovers that Pam's father, Jack prefers to be asked for his daughter's hand in marriage first before the proposal. Greg and Pam take a visit to the Burns home, so that Greg can secretly ask Pam's father for his daughter's hand in marriage, before proposing. Jack is a former agent of the CIA, and through his own experience, and incorrect background check on Greg, has the wrong impression of him and dislikes Greg very much. Against all odds, Greg, must now try to win back Jack's trust and liking, through a visit that just can't be any worse. Through all his efforts of trying to befriend Jack, Greg ends up losing Jack's rare cat, giving Pam's sister a black eye, sets the Burns' garden on fire; just to name a few! Great movie for a gentleman candidate to show him how not to give up, despite the odds against him.

A Father's Rulebook on the Do's and Don'ts for Dating His Little Princess

10 – 100 Dating Ideas

Take your pick! There are 100 dating ideas listed below, with at least one for everyone, hopefully more. To help make your selections easier, they're broken down into sections such as First Date Ideas, Romantic Date Ideas, Outdoor Date Ideas, Indoor Date Ideas and Cheap Date Ideas.

Your date will appreciate the effort you put into a date. The more elaborate, the more they'll like it. Have a date centered around all their favorite things in life. Food, hobbies, talents, or movies, find out through casual conversation, or ask their friends to get the inside scoop, about her likes and dislikes.

First Date Ideas

First dates can be tricky, it's important to give a good first impression. If you're looking to impress your date, plan ahead! Make it a fun, exciting outing your date will never forget. Below are some great first date ideas that are sure to be a hit. Remember, you only get one "first" date!

1. Go to a movie.

2. Carve a pumpkin or watermelon.

3. Shaving cream art on the table with prize for best picture.

4. Sock puppet show.

5. Play broom hockey. It's like hockey, but with brooms.

6. Miniature golf.

7. Play laser tag.

8. Go to the zoo.

9. Have a picnic in the park.

10. Go ride go-carts.

11. Go to an arcade.

12. Go to a car show.

13. Go bowling.

14. Rent a paddle boat or canoe.

15. Watch the stars with a telescope.

16. Go to an IMAX movie.

17. Karaoke.

18. Go listen to a local band.

19. Go to a comedy club, look for a local group, there are a lot of fun comedy groups especially at local universities.

20. Have a costume date, this can be a lot of fun when you go see a movie and dress up like the characters in the movie.

Romantic Date Ideas

Show your date that this is more than just a fun "hang-out" relationship. Below are more fun ideas for spending time with that special

A Father's Rulebook on the Do's and Don'ts for Dating His Little Princess

someone, or your potential special someone. These romantic date ideas are known to cause a severe case of mutual affection.

21. Drive to places you have fond memories of and share them together. It's a good way to get to know each other and make memories of your own.

22. Go for a walk to your favorite ice cream shop in town and eat your ice cream together on a park bench.

23. Take a roll of pennies to a fountain and make wishes out loud as you throw them in.

24. Build a bonfire and roast marshmallows.

25. Go dancing.

26. Gather or take pictures and make a scrap book together.

27. Find a tricky jigsaw puzzle to put together. This is great time to just talk.

28. Walk your dog(s) or borrow a neighbor's dog.

29. Go to a playground and swing on the swings.

30. Rent a tandem bicycle so you can ride together.

31. Lie in the grass and find shapes in the clouds.

32. Go ice or roller skating.

33. Read a book together by the fire or a heat lamp.

34. Take a walk around a ritzy side of town (somewhere with cool lighting, like a strip mall, cool park, or a ritzy neighborhood especially during Christmas time).

35. Go to an old part of town, gas light district (and I don't mean the ghetto or the local gas station). Somewhere with old shops and the cobblestone or brick building kind of feel.

36. Ride a horse-drawn buggy.

37. Go walking in the rain and share an umbrella.

38. Watch the sunrise, watch the sunset.

39. Write poetry and see who can come up with the most original and romantic poetry, G-rated of course.

40. Write a letter, put it in an air-tight bottle and throw it into the ocean or a lake or a river.

Outdoor Date Ideas

Feeling outdoorsy? When the weather is nice, or even when it's not, there are many great things to do outside. Outdoor dates can be a lot of fun, and there are so many options when the weather is nice. Below is a great list of the most exciting things to do outside on a date.

41. Hike to see waterfall or local landmark.

42. Make kites and go to a local park to fly them.

43. Go for a bike ride in your neighborhood.

44. Go to the park and feed the birds.

45. Walk to random spots in your hometown and take pictures together.

46. Build a sand castle. This could be at the beach, or even in a sand box.

47. Glow sticks in a park, need we say more.

48. Go on a nature hike, pick wild flowers.

49. Play Frisbee golf.

50. Play your favorite sport together.

A Father's Rulebook on the Do's and Don'ts for Dating His Little Princess

51. Play capture-the-flag or hide-and-seek in a park.

52. Play croquet at a park, maybe on your school campus grounds.

53. Go fishing.

54. Plant something together, a tree, flowers, vegetable. Anything green!

55. Have a water balloon fight or set up a slip-in-slide.

56. Build a snowman. Have a snowball fight

57. Find a big hill and go sledding.

58. Rent a paddle boat or canoe.

59. Water parks.

60. Try a rock climbing wall.

Indoor Date Ideas

There are more fun things to do on dates indoors. If the weather is contrary, take a look at this list below where weather isn't a problem.

61. Make a movie together. Find old props around the house, then come up with a creative plot to act out.

62. Have a poker tournament but instead of betting money do it with something fun and random like candy or cookies.

63. Make a homemade pizza together then sit down for a candle light dinner and freshly made tossed salad.

64. Go "people watching" at the mall. It can be fun to just sit and talk.

65. Go to your local animal shelter and play with the animals. Who knows, you just might find a new friend.

66. Coloring pictures together is a great indoor date idea. Find a fun coloring book or print coloring book pages off the internet.

67. Finger painting, put on an apron because this can get messy. Find some big paper or maybe a cardboard box and make a masterpiece together.

68. Take a trip to your local hobby shop. Pick out a project to work on for the afternoon, maybe build a boat, or a rocket, something that you both can play with.

69. Read a book together. Choose your favorite childhood story and read aloud.

70. Put on a play and choose a popular story from literature, or a movie.

71. Write a song together.

72. Make life lists together, all the things you want to do before you die.

73. Have a marshmallow eating contest to see who in the group can fit the most in their mouth.

74. Visit a nursing or rest home (assisted living center) and make new friends.

75. Tour historical buildings.

76. Play pool, foosball, or ping-pong.

77. Play guitar hero or rock band.

78. Have a dinner or lunch together with your parents.

79. Walk through the library or a bookstore. Find a corner to sit and read your favorite books together.

80. Go and volunteer together at the local veterans' center.

Cheap Date Ideas

Contrary to popular belief, you really don't have to spend a lot of money to have a great time. Here is a list of ideas for cheap, fun dates, as well as some great free date ideas.

81. Make a time capsule to put in a park or just your own backyard full of pictures and objects that represent your relationship and then dig it up for a big anniversary.

82. Go on an arboretum and discover nature.

83. Try a club activity together.

84. Go to your local coffee shop and just hang out and talk.

85. Draw pictures of each other and show off your artsy side.

86. Play your favorite board games, but don't get bored in the process.

87. Work on an extra credit or homework project together.

88. Take a parks and recreation class or course together.

89. Go visit your local planetarium.

90. Free factory tours.

91. Have a coupon date. Go through the local newspaper of Google for coupons together and find coupons to use on your cheap date.

92. Find a good service project or volunteer activity in your area.

93. Story time, take turns recording pieces of a story.

94. Drive-in movie.

95. Have a scary movie marathon, or just a movie marathon.

96. Go get some white tee-shirts and tie-dye them crazy colors.

97. School sporting events, usually cheap to get into and school spirit is usually high.

98. Go to an art show or exhibit.

99. Go to a museum.

100. Go to a park and bring chalk and decorate the sidewalk with all your amazing art.

Of course, there are plenty more, and you probably have your own favorites, so go with them. My only comment is to make sure they're safe and sane as many of the dating ideas that I came across didn't make this list for that reason.

11 – The 411 on Online Dating

With the advances of the internet, online social sites have become much more popular than before, and it can be very tempting for your daughter to move most of her social life from the real world to the online world.

But the online world has many pitfalls. Some of them are different from the ones in a normal dating relationship. She must be aware that when she's online, it's a different medium, and she has to compensate for the fact that there's much more room to be dishonest online then in real life. She must be extra careful.

Try to take it slow, even with online dating, until you feel like you got to know that person. And use lots of common sense. If you want to move the relationship forward from online dating, the first step is to have a phone conversation because you can tell a lot more about a person through the sound of their voice than you can online. Beware of anyone asking for personal details about yourself, including sensitive and secure information like credit card numbers or social security number or anything like that.

Unsafe Online Dating

Lured by the promise of somebody who appears to understand them, teens can be very naive about the risks of meeting complete strangers on-line and may enjoy the secrecy of such meetings. Smart parents need to ensure that their children understand the risks of such activities. Above all, good parents ensure that their teens don't feel the need to keep secrets from them and teens in turn feel comfortable their parents can keep them safe.

More than a quarter of children using teen dating apps, some as young as thirteen, have been contacted by adults online. An investigation by The Independent, a British newspaper, found a website marketing itself to thirteen to twenty-year-olds breached the rules governing nudity by allowing posts such as: "Do any girls want to post nudes messages" and "Horny girls message me."

A recent survey by ChildLine asked teens under the age of sixteen who used dating sites and apps about their experiences. Of the 400 people who took part, it found as many as 29% admitted they had been in touch with someone over the age of eighteen. Of those, 72% said the person who contacted them online had known their real age. One in five who met someone in person after making contact through the apps said they "felt unsafe" when they saw them face-to-face.

For many young people socializing on the move through mobile phone apps is part of everyday life. So, it's vital that when they sign up to an app they aren't exposed to adult sexual content or have encounters with adults that puts them at risk of being sexually abused.

Digital Media

Access to the internet is nearly universal among adolescents in the United States. Digital media offer opportunities for youth to confidentially search for information on sensitive topics, and thus are a likely source of sexual health information for young people.

Online sources may be particularly important for (lesbian, gay, bisexual, transgender, and queer) LGBTQ adolescents, whose needs may be left out of traditional sex education. The confidentiality of the internet may also be particularly attractive for these adolescents, who may not be comfortable discussing sexual health topics with parents or friends.

In 2010, nineteen percent of heterosexual youth, 40% of questioning youth, 65% of bisexual youth and 78% of lesbian/gay/queer youth aged 13–18 reported that they had used the internet to look up sexual health information in the past year.

Seventy-three percent of adolescents aged 13–17 own a smartphone. More up-to-date research is needed to document how and to what extent adolescents access and utilize sexual health information online with smartphones and other digital media and devices.

Digital media, including social networking sites, apps and text messaging services, are increasingly being used to reach adolescents with sexual health interventions, and studies have demonstrated efficacy in improving knowledge and behavior across a range of sexual health outcomes.

The websites adolescents may turn to for sexual health information often have inaccurate information. For example, of 177 sexual health websites examined in a recent study, 46% of those addressing contraception and 35% of those addressing abortion contained inaccurate information.

Social Media Networking Sites Teens are Using

If your daughter is intent on using on-line dating or social media sites to chat with boys and eventually go out on a date, you should check them out yourself if you have the slightest doubt they're not abiding by their security features, age restrictions, and living up to your dating standards.

Stay informed about what your teen is up to in the online world, even though it's hard to keep up much of the time. Educate yourself about which social media sites your teen is using so you can establish clear guidelines and expectations. Although many social networking sites seem to come and go, here are some of the places where you can find teens lately:

➢ Ask.fm

So You Want to Date My Daughter?

- Bebo
- Chatpit
- Classmates
- Facebook
- Flickr
- Fun Date City
- Google
- Instagram
- Knuddels
- MeetMe
- Meetup
- MyLOL
- OurTeenNetwork
- Pinterest
- Reddit
- Skype
- Snapchat
- Teen Chat
- TeenSay
- Tumblr
- Twitter

- Vine Camera
- VK
- WeChat
- YouTube
- Zoosk

Ten Social Media Damage Protection Strategies

The vast majority of teens are using at least one of these social networking sites and no doubt others that haven't made the list above. Although social media can offer many educational opportunities, it can also be very dangerous for teens as previously noted. Establish rules about social media to keep your teen emotionally and physically safe and be aware of the following.

Educate Yourself About Social Media

Develop a good understanding of what your teen is doing on social media. Educate yourself about various social media sites and know which sites your teen frequents. Learn about the risks associated with various social media sites so you can have meaningful conversations

View Your Teen's Privacy Settings

Each social media site has different rules about privacy settings. View your teen's privacy settings and discuss the possible implications of making information public. Be aware that some social media sites make it difficult for teens to keep their information private.

Provide Education on How to Respond to Inappropriate Behavior

Unfortunately, it's common for teens to be approached by adults online. Sometimes, they are shown pornographic material or asked to engage in sexual conversations. Discuss how you expect your teen to respond and act if problems like these should develop. Make it clear that your child won't get into trouble for notifying you and explain the importance of talking about it so that you can work together to find ways to prevent it from happening again.

Talk About What's Appropriate to Share

Engage in frequent conversations about what is appropriate to share on social media and what isn't. Sometimes teens need reminders that they shouldn't say things online that they wouldn't say to someone's face. Make it clear that there can be serious ramifications for bullying, making threats, or engaging in sexualized behavior via social media.

Establish Clear Rules About Respecting Everyone's Privacy

Make it clear that your teen shouldn't be airing your family's private affairs or posting embarrassing photos or information about anyone else. Establish a rule that says no photographs or information about others can be posted. Otherwise, teens can end up using social media as a weapon against one another or parents are embarrassed to hear that their personal information is now public.

Keep Tabs on Your Teen's Social Media Use

Sometimes parents struggle over whether or not they should have all of their teen's social media passwords. Parents should take this on a case-by-case basis. It may be appropriate to do so when teens engage in unsafe behavior or when they aren't yet mature enough to handle privacy on social media. Even if you don't have your teen's passwords, take steps to keep an eye on what your teen is doing on social media. At the very least, view your teen's public social media pages to see what it is being publicized to the world.

Warn Your Teen About Scams

Teens need to know about potential ways they could be taken advantage of on social media. Explain how some people are tricked into giving out their personal information and how others are scammed into giving away money. Also discuss how people online are not always who they claim to be. Talk to your teen about news stories that show how people got themselves into trouble due to various online scams and continue to make it a frequent topic of conversation.

Discuss How Social Media can Impact Their Future

It's important for teens to realize that colleges and future employers are going to be looking at their social media activity. Explain how inappropriate comments and photos can come back to haunt them years later. Make it clear that once something is shared on the internet, it will remain in cyberspace and people may be able to access it forever.

Encourage Teens to Think Before They Share

Teens are impulsive by nature and posting a hasty social media message can lead to trouble. Encourage your teen to always think about what they're posting and to prevent them from impulsively reacting to others. Help your teen develop a plan that will prevent her from doing and saying things she may later regret.

Set Time Limits on Social Media Use

It can be easy to lose track of time on the internet, especially when using social media. Set time limits to prevent your teen from spending hours on the internet. Most pediatricians recommend no more than two hours of screen time per day.

How to Prevent Social Media Abuse

Parents should also reinforce the permanence of their electronic interactions and the possibility it could impact their future. Anything sent or posted in cyberspace never truly goes away, even when deleted. A naked or suggestive picture taken and sent can never be taken back. It may seem fun and flirty at the time, but once someone else has it, it is impossible to control.

The boyfriend your daughter adores may become the ex who hates her and then posts her picture for all to see. Even if that doesn't happen, any message your teen sends can be later seen by potential employers, college recruiters, teachers, coaches, family, friends, enemies, and strangers. Remind your teen not to forward any photos they receive; they should simply delete them.

Talk to Your Teen About Sexting

Texting is a favorite pastime of the current generation of teenagers. Although it can be a great way of staying in touch with family and friends, it does have pitfalls.

One of the problems arising from texting is something called "sexting." Sexting is sending sexually explicit messages or photos via cell phone or instant messenger. Many teens are engaging in sexting and don't realize the impact it can have on their lives. The problem lies with how quickly our technology can spread that material. Messages, photos or videos sent privately can easily be shared with others. Once digital images are sent, they leave a footprint and cannot be taken back.

Surveys show that 40% of teens are engaged in some sort of sexting, whether that's initiating it or just being the unsuspecting recipient of an explicit photo. It's happening, and teens are keeping quiet about it. While you may think your child would never do something like that, you might be surprised what they are sending via texts. It's important to talk about sexting as soon as you hand your teen their own cell phone.

Besides defining what sexting is, it's important to explain the difference between flirting and sexting. People, in general, are more apt to text something inappropriate than to say it to someone's face, so teens can quickly get on a slippery slope where flirting leads to sexting. Be sure to tell your teenager that flirting is when you pay attention to someone you like and say nice things. Any message that implies intimacy, such as referring to undergarments, sexual acts, or photos of anything you wouldn't do in public, is inappropriate, and parents should make it clear this is unacceptable.

Finally, be sure to warn your teen that some states have laws in place that consider any copy of a sexually explicit picture of a teen as child pornography, which means that a teen who received a photo from another teen could potentially be prosecuted and have a record as a sex offender.

Damaged Reputations

The sum of all your daughter's social-media activity is an electronic reflection of her. Make sure it's a true reflection of who she really is.

Think of her reputation like a company or organizations would think of their collective brand, so it's critical she manages it all with that purpose in mind. Her behavior on social media becomes her brand and builds upon her reputation. While the digital world is her platform, she must use it with care because there is a fine line between productive and destructive behavior.

Be careful about what she posts, be cautious about the photos she publishes, and be purposeful about who she lets into her circle. Her reputation is built upon every social media interaction, so she should be consistent and ladylike with it with the friends and followers she keeps and has gathered in her social media lifetime.

Even the people she follows can reflect upon her reputation, so she should be conscious that every "like" or "dislike" could have ramifications. Remember that it's all a permanent record; once someone else shares what you posted, it's been published into the world.

There's a reason they call the world wide web, so make sure she manages her social media reputation just like the big brands do, and not like a Kardashian!

12 – Chaperoning, Proms, Parties and Driving

During her formative dating years, there must be a balance between not setting too many restrictions that prevent your daughter from experience dating, to one where there is little, or no parental supervision and your teenager can pretty much date and do as she please.

While your daughter is still under your care, guidance, and parental authority, parents have the opportunity to help ensure what happens during dates, proms, and parties stays respectable and decent and doesn't get out of control. As a dad, you're the guardian of morality.

Now that you've seen the good, the bad, and the ugly in dating candidates as well as the multitude of things that can go wrong on a date, this chapter enlightens dads and parents on the power of chaperoning their daughter's proms and dances, parties and events, and ensuring safe and sane driving habits in the process.

A chaperone is usually an adult who supervises tweens and teenagers during social occasions and dates. Usually, it's the father, mother, aunt, or anybody who acts as a guardian. Chaperones are there to prevent any inappropriate social or sexual interactions on a date or event as well as make sure there is no illegal behavior such as drug use or underage drinking.

Furthermore, once your daughter has her driver's license, she has a lot more independence and freedom to go where she wants. However, you can still set limits on when she drives, where to, with whom, and how often. There are also ways to track where she goes and where she's been if needed.

It's your choice dad: Do you want to be more in control of your daughter's dating years, or controlled by it? You can choose to be a proactive or reactive parent. Proactive parents set rules, boundaries, and expectations regarding safe and sane dating practices and reactive parents don't. The ones that don't can suffer for it along with their daughters and ultimately pay the price for them.

Chaperoning Proms and Dances

What is it about prom night that sends parents into a fit of fear? Is it memories of our own proms (and the debauched parties we attended)? Or maybe visions of the entire second half of the John Hughes classic, "Sixteen Candles?"

The senior prom is an American high school tradition that most teens anxiously wait for. And one of the main reasons for this is the most highly anticipated night of having sex. More teenagers will get pregnant on this night that on any other and the peer pressure to have sex is enormous.

The excitement on that night, the anticipation, her anxiety, and feeling of nostalgia that come along with memorable moments like this one can certainly affect the way she feels about a situation and affect her better judgment. So, before you let your daughter check into a hotel room after the prom, consider other options for after prom activities like the ones discussed later in this chapter.

Like most parents, you want to be a part of every milestone in your teenager's life, but when it comes to going to the prom, knowing the potential ramifications, should you let your teen have this moment to herself or should you volunteer to be a prom chaperone?

School dances are common for high schools and even some middle schools, so here are some tips on how to be a chaperone without keeping your child or teen from having fun.

Discuss Being a Prom Chaperone with Your Teen

Chaperoning a prom is something that should be approached with special care and consideration. Approach your teen with your desire to lend a hand at his prom and see how she feels about the idea. Prom is considered a rite of passage for most teens and as they prepare to finish high school, it is important to show your trust and respect for this stage in their life.

When determining how your presence at the prom will affect your relationship with your teen, take a look at recent interactions you have had: Does your child invite you to be a part of activities with friends or do they run the other way when they see you coming? Don't take it personally if the latter is true. Some teens may be mortified of the thought of having a parent at prom; others may hardly notice you are there.

Is your teen hesitant about mom and dad hanging around their senior prom? Discuss options for volunteering. Helping out doesn't mean you have to go to the prom during the event. However, when your need to go to the prom stems from trust issues with your teen, consider asking an aunt or trusted adult to attend in your place.

So, should you chaperone your teen's prom? Ultimately, the decision to go to the prom as a prom chaperone should be made in partnership with your teen. Although it may seem like your little princess' youth has flashed by when she shows resistance to the idea of her parents crashing her senior prom, respect her feelings and know there will be other milestones in which you can be front and center.

How to Be a Good Chaperone

The most important rule is to treat your teen like you wanted to be treated at their age. They're not children any longer; they're young adults and would like to be treated as such. This isn't the time to take pictures either, take them before your teenager leaves the house instead.

Keep in mind that your teen may ignore you or avoid you while you're there. That's to be expected since they're trying to spread their wings and learn to be more independent. They need to be able to have fun without worrying about you checking up on them. However, your teen may have feelings of resentment about your attendance at their senior prom. And there's always the possibility that other parents may expect you to "spy" on their children.

It's best to stay out of your child's way and to keep a low profile. You'll want to have your own way to and from the dance because your teen probably won't want to be seen with you. You'll also want to wear something fashionable but understated so you don't compete with the students. Dads can wear a suit but don't have to wear a tie.

Remember why you're at the prom. You're not there to spy on your daughter or to keep her from having fun. Your priority is to ensure that all of the students at the dance are safe. Follow the instructions you were given about enforcing the school's policies. Don't accept or tolerate inappropriate behavior from anyone, including your own daughter.

You're not there to dance, so do everything you can to keep from doing so, no matter how much the music makes you want to bust out a move. Please resist the urge as if your life depends upon it; it just might if your teen catches you dancing and gets embarrassed in front of their friends.

Freak Dancing at School Dances

Many daughters no longer want to attend their high school dances because of all the freak dancing that goes on. They find it distasteful to have to fend off would-be freak dance partners and it takes the thrill out of attending and enjoying the social aspect of dancing.

Your child should be able to go to her school dances without feeling intimidated by the type of dancing there and need to know this form of dancing will not be tolerated. Granted some teens think they are cool dancing in that manner, but you have to ask them, "What kind of message do you want to give your peers when you are on your knees simulating having oral sex at the dance or pretending to be having back door intercourse?"

At some private schools, they prevent this by making a time out room. Yes, a time out room! If you dance like that you get sent to the time out room for half an hour of the dance. If you get sent twice in one year you lose the privileges of going to the school dance. This has been done at public schools as well.

Boycotting the Prom for Personal Reasons and Preferences

For parents of teenage daughters where proms and dancing might conflict with their religious, moral, or sexual preference. or maybe when your daughter doesn't have a date, doesn't want one, or thinks the prom and dances are overblown and not for them, there may be other options below more to their liking.

- ➢ Invite your daughter's friends over for a party at your house on a night other than the prom night, when they are available.

- ➢ Offer to give your daughter a night to remember. Do something with her that she's never done before. For example: Take her on a dinner cruise the night of the prom. Let her invite her friends so she can celebrate with them.

- ➢ Offer to take her to an amusement park for the whole day. Let her invite her friends.

- ➢ Do a daddy-daughter day. For example: Spend the day with your daughter at a salon, then go shopping, and go to a restaurant.

A Father's Rulebook on the Do's and Don'ts for Dating His Little Princess

- Take her to a place she's never been to before. For example: On top of the Empire State Building in New York, and then explore New York.

- Visit a university or college campus with her. Let her speak to the students there. Many universities have welcoming committees to show perspective students around campus. Don't forget to visit the student center.

- Send her to visit her favorite relative for a few days.

- Give her a special graduation present. Something she's wanted for a long time.

- Give her a slumber party night at a hotel with her friends. Give her a choice of chaperones.

- Offer her a limousine tour of the town with her friends.

These are just a few ideas. If you sit down and discuss them with your daughter, she should be able to come up with several of your own. Most daughters will appreciate your help with making sure she doesn't feel left out from proms and dances. For many, the alternates may be more fun and turn out to be better!

Consider Hosting a Party After the Prom

Knowing the peer pressure and opportunities to have sex after the prom, there are better options for your daughter spending the night in a hotel room after the prom. Teenagers have come to expect a hotel room after the prom because parents have allowed hotel rooms after the prom. You can stop this unsafe tradition. It doesn't have to be that way!

After the prom, parents or a community may host a "prom afterparty" or "afterglow" or "post-prom" at a restaurant, entertainment venue, or a student's home. Other traditions often include trips to nearby attractions, such as amusement parks, regional or local parks, or family or rented vacation houses. Many post prom events are at the school, and involve bringing entertainment such as interactive games, artists, and other entertainers to the school.

Lay out the expectation before the start of any of these events that illegal substances for a minor are not permitted. Sometimes parents think it is cool to provide alcohol at these events, but underage drinking is illegal, and parents are legally responsible for the teen behavior and use of illegal substances.

Parties

There comes a time when your daughter wants to throw a party at your house or attend a house party somewhere else where there are no adults present. Any party for tweens and teens with no parents present, no matter the location, whether it's your house or another, is unacceptable. There must be a responsible parent present during the party at all times. As a responsible parent, you need to have the current contact info of the parent of the teen that is hosting the party.

Don't let your daughter change your position on this because she says, "you're way too strict and many of my friends have parties without parents in the home all the time!" This is a common problem and too often the seriousness is underestimated or dismissed with a shrug.

Even some of the most reliable teens can be coerced into taking advantage of a house party when there are no adults present, particularly if it's their house. There will be times when you have to muster all the forces and show you're serious about maintaining these rules. Don't give in!

Unsupervised Teen Parties

What typically happens during a house party unattended by an adult? Kids show-up that were uninvited! There are lots of illegal substances! There is loud and offensive music! There is a fight or disturbance outside! Things are broken or stolen! There is sexual activity of one degree or another taking place! Things get out of control! And so, and so, and so on!

If you're on vacation, out of town, on a business trip, etc. and your teenage daughter is going to be home alone, there are things you can do ahead of time to make sure she's safe. The first is to have her stay at her most reliable friend's house and work out an agreement with their parents (or parent), about the stay over and sleep over. If you have a big or extended family, you might be able to get one of them to stay at your house while you're gone.

If neither option is available and your teen is going to be home alone, be prepared for the worst-case scenario, a house party! The temptation is irresistible, especially if she has a boyfriend. No matter how much she reassures you "nothing like that is going to happen," think back to your teenage years and remember when you had a house party, or your friends did, and there was a "betrayal of our trust" when it did happen. House parties happen to the best of kids and more often to the worst of them. So be prepared!

If none of the options above will work for you, consider these:

- ➢ Get an alarm system that connects to a monitoring service that will send out a security alert if for any reason your daughter is threatened or there's an emergency.

- ➢ Have a neighbor, friend, or relative check up on your daughter and encourage them to call the police if anything suspicious happens.

- ➢ Alert the police that you'll be away, but not your daughter, and ask them to make an extra drive by at night in case there's a party going on.

Options for Dealing with Other Parties and Illegal Substances

Below are some sound rules for dealing with parties that your daughter may be going to. There are also rules in the next section for a house party she's throwing at her house that you've sanctioned and will be there as the responsible adult.

No parties allowed without communication with parental hosts. It's critical you get all contact info; name, home and cell phone numbers, and e-mail address if possible.

Parent hosts send out a notice or announcement via parent listserv or email list (compiled outside of school) notifying of time, date, and address of the party.

Parents adopt "risk management" and "risk reduction" strategies for their parties in order to prevent drug and alcohol use, sexual misconduct, random acts of stupidity, etc.

Parents use a "no questions asked" policy or "get out of jail free" card where they pick up their child, or another, and take them home safely because they were at a party that night, might be driving under the influence, or be in a car with someone under the influence, etc. However, it's unreasonable to expect that parents won't pursue the issue when all participants are sober and awake, and things have calmed down.

Hosting a Teen Party

Hosting a teen party is not for the weak of heart. It takes a lot of prep and even the strong of heart need to have anywhere from two or more adults present to help them depending on the party's size. Even with full parental supervision, take the following precautions.

Be clear with your teen about the invitation process. Make it very specific and discrete and creating a list for you to use in admitting people. Even then, think about how you'll plan to handle uninvited guests.

Provide secure locations in your house, car, or safe where you can hide and lock up all alcohol and all contents of medicine cabinets, and any valuable belongings. An "out of sight" and "out of mind policy" helps reduce temptation.

Don't expect to be able to control every movement and whereabouts of your guests. They have a tendency to roam; however, you should make all guests aware of the house rules on where they can and cannot go to.

Teenage Driving and Safety

It's true that once your daughter has her driver's license, she has a lot more independence and the freedom to go where she wants. But you can still set limits on when she drives, where she drives to, who she drives with, and how often.

Before she starts driving, it's a good idea for parents to discuss the new changes in the law (if there any in your state) with their teens and emphasize that the changes will enable them to become better drivers while reducing their exposure to risky driving situations that they might not be ready to handle.

New and Revised Driving Laws

In most states, after you pass your driving test, you'll be issued a provisional driver license. In 1997, California was the first state to pass a Graduated Driver's License (GDL) law that included a passenger limit for teen drivers. In the first two years after passage of the law, teen passengers killed and injured in crashes involving sixteen-year-old drivers decreased by 40%. The same study showed that teen drivers with passengers were significantly more at risk of causing a crash than solo teen drivers.

Provisional Driver License

With a provisional driver license, teenage drivers must be accompanied and supervised by some 25 years of age or older, or by a licensed or certified driving instructor when they:

> ➤ Transport passengers under twenty years of age at any time, for the first twelve months.

> ➤ Drive between 11 p.m. and 5 a.m. for the first twelve months.

This means your teen cannot give anyone under twenty years old her friend(s), brother(s), sister(s), cousin(s), etc. a ride unless you have a licensed parent, a guardian or other adult 25 years old or older in the car with you.

You are also not allowed to drive between 11 p.m. and 5 a.m. during their first year after getting their license unless they have a licensed parent, a guardian or other adult 25 years old or older in the car with them.

Teen Driving Restrictions

An analysis by the Traffic Injury Research Foundation of teen crash rates indicates that the injury crash risk to both teen drivers and underage passengers significantly declines each month after licensing, then stabilizes a little more than one year after drivers first receive their licenses.

Teen drivers with less than one year of experience may still carry passengers under age twenty as long as there is an adult 25 or older in the vehicle. Young family members can also be transported without having an adult in the car. The 11 p.m. driving curfew also contains exceptions for work and school attendance.

All the provisions of the Graduated Driver's License (GDL) law are enforced as secondary violations, that is, a law enforcement officer must first pull over a driver for another possible infraction before the driver will be cited for a violation of the GDL law.

Active and Passive Teen Tracking Devices

An active GPS personal monitoring tracking device allows you to monitor a vehicle at all times. You can see where it is in real time. You can also look at history; where the vehicle was, how long it was there, how fast it was going. Active GPS teen tracking can notify you if the vehicle is involved in an accident or if it leaves a specific geographic area.

A passive tracking system records the history of a vehicle. That history can later be downloaded and reviewed. You cannot locate a vehicle in real time with a passive system. It does tell you where a vehicle was and for how long and the speeds at which it was traveling.

Teenage Driver Accident Statistics

The per mile crash rate for teenaged drivers is three times higher after 9 p.m. than during the day. This is because the task of driving at night is more difficult; they have less experience driving at night than during the day; they are more sleep deprived, and/or because teenage recreational driving, which often involves alcohol, is more likely to occur at night.

- New teen drivers have twice the rate of car accidents of older drivers.

- Fifty-percent of fatal teen-driver accidents occur after dark, even though only 20% of teen driving occurs at night.

- Crash risks (even for sober teens) increase exponentially with numbers of passengers. One passenger equals a 50% increase in the likelihood of a crash. Two passengers bring the likelihood to 200%. Three or more, the risk increases by 300 to 500%!

- The crash rate for sixteen-year-olds is 3.7 times higher than drivers of all ages.

- The citation rate for sixteen-year-olds is 1.8 times higher than drivers of all ages.

- The crash rate for 16 - 19-year-olds is 2.7 times higher than drivers of all ages.

- The citation rate for 16 - 19-year-olds is 2.1 times higher than drivers of all ages.

- The has been drinking (HBD) crash rate for sixteen-year-old drivers is 1.8 times higher than drivers of all ages.

- The HBD crash rate for 16 - 19-year-old drivers is 1.9 times higher than drivers of all ages.

Prom Night Driving Statistics

Now add in these staggering prom night numbers from a survey of 11th and 12th graders conducted by MADD (Mothers Against Drunk Driving) and the Chrysler Corporation. When asked about their upcoming prom night, the teenagers reported that:

- 50% will drive themselves and a date; 25% will drive four or more passengers (meaning a three-to five-fold increased crash risk).

- 86% of the drivers will drive after midnight; 50% after 2 a.m.

- 74% reported pressure to drink that night; 49% felt pressed to do other drugs.

- 57% felt pressured to drive recklessly (i.e. speeding or ignoring traffic signals to act cool).

13 – A Sex Education Primer

Our youth today are growing up in a culture that surrounds them with sexual imagery and messages, but one in which marriage is often delayed until the late twenties or later.

Historically, public health prevention messages have singled out abstinence until marriage as the most effective way to remain free of sexually transmitted diseases (STDs) and recently classified as sexually transmitted infections (STIs). Yet while abstinence is a fundamentally important aspect of preventing STDs and STIs, this message alone does not serve well in the absence of comprehensive sexual education and a supportive environment.

"Formal" sexual health education is instruction that generally takes place in a structured setting, such as a school, youth center, church or other community-based location. This type of instruction is a central source of information for adolescents. Young people deserve balanced, accurate, and realistic sex education, as well as access to confidential sexual health services.

What Are the Goals of Sex Education for Youth?

Sex education is designed to help young people gain the information, skills and motivation to make healthy decisions about sex and sexuality throughout their lives.

Is Sex Education Effective?

Research on sex education has focused on whether programs help young people to change specific behaviors related to preventing pregnancy and sexually transmitted diseases such as:

- ➢ Delaying sex until they are older.
- ➢ Using condoms and contraception when they do have sex.
- ➢ Reducing the frequency of sex.
- ➢ Reducing the number of sexual partners.

Hundreds of studies have shown that sex education can have a positive effect on these behaviors, particularly when sex education programs incorporate all of the following seventeen key characteristics as developed by Douglas Kirby from the National Campaign to Prevent Teen and Unplanned Pregnancy:

What's the State of Sex Education in the U.S.?

There is broad public support for sex education programs, but many young people are still not receiving the sex education they need. Sex Education is widely supported by the vast majority of people in the United States. In Planned Parenthood's most recent poll on sex education, 93% of parents supported having sex education taught in middle school, and 96% of parents supported having sex education taught in high school.

The vast majority of parents support sex education in middle school and high school that covers a wide range of topics, including STDs, puberty, healthy relationships, contraception, and sexual orientation. Other national, state and local polls on sex education have shown similarly high levels of support.

Federal & State Policy Related to Sex Education

Sex Education programming varies widely across the United States. Currently, 24 states and the District of Columbia mandate sex education and 34 states mandate HIV education. Although almost every state has some guidance on how and when sex education should be taught, decisions are often left up to individual school districts.

Planned Parenthood plays an important role in advocating for federal funding for evidence-based programming such as the Teen Pregnancy Prevention Program (TPP) and the Personal Responsibility Education Program (PREP).

What Sex Education Do Teens Get in the US?

The gap between the sex education students should receive and what they actually receive is wide. According to the 2014 CDC School Health Profiles, fewer than half of high schools and only a fifth of middle schools teach all sixteen topics recommended by the CDC as essential components of sex education. These topics range from basic information on how HIV and other STDs are transmitted, and how to prevent infection, to critical communication and decision-making skills.

In fact, today fewer young people report receiving any formal sex education at all. A recent study published by the Guttmacher Institute found that fewer teens now than in the past are being exposed to important and timely information about a range of sex education topics. Overall, in 2011–2013, 43% of adolescent females and 57% of adolescent males did not receive information about birth control before they had sex for the first time. Despite these declines in formal education, there was no increase in the proportion of teens who discussed these same sex education topics with their parents.

Comprehensive Sex Ed

Research clearly shows that comprehensive sex education programs do not encourage teens to start having sexual intercourse, do not increase the frequency with which teens have intercourse, and do not increase the number of a teen's sexual partners. Research also shows that sex education programs that promote abstinence only have in fact proven ineffective.

Why Is Sexual Education Taught in Schools?

Sex education in the United States is taught in two main forms: comprehensive sex education and abstinence-only. Comprehensive sex education covers abstinence as a choice option, but also informs adolescents about human sexuality, age of consent and the availability of contraception and techniques to avoid contraction of sexually transmitted infections. Abstinence-only sex education emphasizes abstinence from sexual activity prior to marriage and rejects methods such as contraception. The difference between the two approaches, and their impact on the behavior of adolescents, remains a controversial subject in the United States.

Soaring rates of sexually transmitted diseases among teens are adding urgency to the debate over sex education. Conservatives claim the alarming statistics illustrate why abstinence should be the single mantra when it comes to sex ed. Liberals counter that the increase in disease is the strongest case for more detailed information. Caught in the middle are America's kids, who are more vulnerable than ever to potentially deadly diseases.

The Sex Ed Debate

In the debate over sex education, one thing is undisputed: The average kid today is immersed in sexual imagery. A generation that has grown up on the sordid details of the Starr Report, watched thong-clad teens gyrate on Spring Break cable specials, or read the cover of nearly any women's magazine in the grocery check-out line is familiar with the facts of life.

But young people face a barrage of confusing messages. Along with titillating images from the media, some kids are told to "just say no" to sex. In school, others are taught how to put condoms on bananas in preparation for the real thing, and still other children receive no information whatsoever.

Transcending the Cacophony of Mixed Messages

Kids are becoming more sexually active at an earlier age. Sixty-six percent of American high school students have had sex by their senior year. And these same teens are paying the price by contracting dangerous, and sometimes deadly, sexually transmitted diseases and infections.

According to the Centers for Disease Control and the Kaiser Family Foundation, approximately 65% of all sexually transmitted infections contracted by Americans this year will occur in people under 24. One in four new HIV infections occurs in people younger than 22.

"There's a disconnect somewhere. Someone's not getting the message. We need to find out why and help our kids be more responsible," said Dr. Ted Feinberg, assistant executive director of the National Association of School Psychologists. But what message should be given to young people is the subject of intense debate.

How Much to Teach?

One side in the debate favors comprehensive sex education, including detailed information about sexually transmitted diseases, contraception and abstinence. The opposing side pushes for an abstinence-only message that advises teens to wait until marriage. Since there is no federal law that requires public schools to teach sex education, let alone one that specifies what should be taught, these decisions are left up to states and individual school districts.

"Young people are going to learn about sex and our question has to be where do we want them to learn? From the media? From their friends? Or do we want them to learn from an educated, responsible adult?" said Tamara Kreinin, President of the Sexuality Information and Education Council of the United States, a leading advocate of comprehensive sex education.

Mixed Signals

A key issue in the battle over sex education is whether giving kids more information about sex and if it actually leads to sexual activity. In a study of 35 sex education programs around the world, the World Health Organization found there is no evidence that comprehensive programs encourage sexual activity.

The study also concluded that abstinence-only programs are less effective than comprehensive classes that include abstinence and safe-sex practices such as contraception and condom use. Related nationwide studies by the Guttmacher Institute and Planned Parenthood came to similar conclusions.

But abstinence-only groups dismiss these studies as biased and skewed. They argue there is a fundamental flaw in giving kids more information about risky behaviors that they should simply be taught to avoid.

Looking for a Balance

Despite all the disagreement, there is some middle ground in the debate. Advocates of comprehensive sex education say the abstinence-only message ignores information critical for teens to protect their health. But they are not against the abstinence message itself.

While activists argue over the right balance, reports show that American parents want some sort of sex education taught in public schools. A 1999 survey conducted by Hickman-Brown Research Inc. found that 93% of all Americans believe sex education should be taught in high schools, and 84% believe it should be taught in middle or junior high schools.

Effectiveness of Formal Sex Education Programs

Leading public health and medical professional organizations, including the American Medical Association; the American Academy of Pediatrics; the American College of Obstetricians and Gynecologists;

the American Public Health Association; the Health and Medicine Division of the National Academies of Science, Engineering, and Medicine (formerly the Institute of Medicine); the American School Health Association and the Society for Adolescent Health and Medicine, support comprehensive sex education.

Strong evidence suggests that approaches to sex education that include information about <u>both</u> contraception and abstinence help young people to delay sex, and also to have healthy relationships and avoid STDs and unintended pregnancies when they do become sexually active. Many of these programs have resulted in delayed sexual debut, reduced frequency of sex and number of sexual partners, increased condom or contraceptive use, or reduced sexual risk-taking.

Abstinence education programs that promote abstinence-only-until-marriage, now termed "sexual risk avoidance" by proponents, have been described as "scientifically and ethically problematic." They systematically ignore or stigmatize many young people and do not meet their health needs.

Research finds that programs that promote abstinence until marriage while withholding information about contraceptive methods do not stop or even delay sex. Moreover, abstinence-only-until-marriage programs can actually place young people at increased risk of pregnancy and STIs.

Most evaluations of sexual health programs focus on reducing levels of adolescent pregnancy, STIs and the behaviors that lead to them. But the broader goal of comprehensive sex education is to support young people's development into sexually healthy adults.

Other Sources of Sexual Health Information

Adolescents may receive information about sexual health topics from a range of sources beyond formal instruction. Here we consider the role of parents, health care providers and digital media as potential sources of sexual health information for adolescents.

Parents

In 2011–2013, 70% of males and 78% of females aged 15 - 19 reported having talked with a parent about at least one of six sex education topics: how to say no to sex, methods of birth control, STDs, where to get birth control, how to prevent HIV infection and how to use a condom.

Young women were more likely than young men to talk with their parents about each of these sexual health topics except how to use a condom, which was more commonly discussed among males (45%) than among females (36%). Although most parents provide information about contraception or other sexual health topics, their knowledge of these topics may be inaccurate or incomplete.

Health Care Providers

Both the American Medical Association and the American Academy of Pediatrics recommend that adolescents' primary care visits include time alone with health care providers to discuss sexuality and receive counseling about sexual behavior. The American College of Obstetricians and Gynecologists advises that contraceptive counseling be included in every visit with adolescents, including those who are not yet sexually active.

Despite these recommendations, only 45% of young people aged 15 - 17 reported in 2013–2015 that they spent time alone with a doctor or other health care provider during their most recent visit in the previous year.

Many health care providers do not talk with their adolescent patients about sexual health issues during primary care visits. When these conversations do occur, they are usually brief; in one study, conversations with patients aged 12 – 17 lasted an average of 36 seconds.

Many adolescents feel uncomfortable talking with their health care provider about sexual health issues, and many providers also have concerns about discussing these issues. Among females aged 15 - 17 who had ever had sex, those who reported concerns about confidentiality were one-third as likely to have received a contraceptive service in the previous year than those who did not have these concerns.

Many young people fall through the information cracks. Among adolescents aged 15 - 19 who had ever had sex and who did not get birth control instruction from either formal sources or a parent, only seven percent of females and thirteen percent of males talked with a health care provider about birth control in 2006–2010.

14 – Adolescence Development and Behavior

Parents are often worried or confused by the physical and mental changes in their teenagers as they go through adolescence. The following information should help parents understand this phase of development. Each teenager is an individual with a unique personality and special interests, likes, and dislikes. However, there are also numerous developmental issues that everyone faces during the adolescent years.

Stages of Adolescence Development

Adolescence is divided into three stages: early (10 to 12 years), middle (13 to 18 years), and late (19 to 21 years). While certain attitudes, behaviors, and physical milestones tend to occur at certain ages, a wide range of growth and behavior for each age is normal. These guidelines show general progress through the developmental stages rather than fixed requirements. It is perfectly natural for a teen to reach some milestones earlier and other milestones later than the general trend.

Early Adolescence (Approximately 10 – 12 Years of Age)

This is a time of many physical, mental, emotional, and social changes. Hormones change as puberty begins. Most boys grow facial and pubic hair and their voices deepen. Most girls grow pubic hair and breasts and start their period. They might be worried about these changes and how they are looked at by others. This also will be a time when your teen might face peer pressure to use alcohol, tobacco products, drugs, and to have sex. Other challenges can be eating disorders, depression, and family problems.

At this age, teens make more of their own choices about friends, sports, studying, and school. They become more independent, with their own personality and interests, although parents are still very important. Most noticeable during this phase are the following attributes:

- Puberty: grow body hair, increase perspiration and oil production in hair and skin.
- Girls breast and hip development, onset of menstruation.
- Boys growth in testicles and penis, wet dreams, deepening of voice.
- Tremendous physical growth: gain height and weight.
- Greater sexual interest.
- Growing capacity for abstract thought.
- Mostly interested in present with limited thought to the future.
- Intellectual interests expand and become more important.
- Deeper moral thinking.
- Struggle with sense of identity.
- Feel awkward about one's self and one's body; worry about being normal.
- Realize that parents are not perfect; increased conflict with parents.

- Increased influence of peer group.
- Desire for independence.
- Tendency to return to "childish" behavior, particularly when stressed.
- Moodiness.
- Rule and limit testing.
- Greater interest in privacy.

Middle Adolescence (Approximately 13 – 18 Years of Age)

This is a time of changes for how teenagers think, feel, and interact with others, and how their bodies grow. Most girls will be physically mature by now, and most will have completed puberty. Boys might still be maturing physically during this time. Your teen might have concerns about body size, shape, or weight. Eating disorders also can be common, especially among girls.

During this time, your teen is developing their unique personality and opinions. Relationships with friends are still important, yet your teen will have other interests as he develops a clearer sense of who he is. This is also an important time to prepare for more independence and responsibility; many teenagers start working, and many will be leaving home soon after high school. Most noticeable during this phase are the following attributes:

- Puberty is completed.
- Physical growth slows for girls, continues for boys.
- Continued growth of capacity for abstract thought.
- Greater capacity for setting goals.
- Interest in moral reasoning.

- Thinking about the meaning of life.

- Intense self-involvement, changing between high expectations and poor self-concept.

- Continued adjustment to changing body, worries about being normal.

- Tendency to distance selves from parents, continued drive for independence.

- Driven to make friends and greater reliance on them, popularity can be an important issue.

- Feelings of love and passion.

Late Adolescence (Approximately 19 – 21 Years of Age)

By this stage, late adolescents are completing their adjustment to a sexually maturing body and feelings. With the significant changes in adolescence, youth must adapt sexually and establish a sense of sexual identity. This includes incorporating a personal sense of masculinity or femininity into one's personal identity; establishing values about sexual behavior; and developing skills for romantic relationships.

Late adolescents should have a clear sexual identity and be concerned with serious relationships and their potential for emotional and physical intimacy. Serious intimate relationships begin to develop. Majority regard love, fidelity and lifelong commitment as very important to a successful relationship. Most are sexually experienced. Most noticeable during this phase are the following attributes:

- Young women, typically, are fully developed.

- Young men continue to gain height, weight, muscle mass, and body hair.

- Ability to think ideas through.

- Ability to delay gratification.
- Examination of inner experiences.
- Increased concern for future.
- Continued interest in moral reasoning.
- Firmer sense of identity.
- Increased emotional stability.
- Increased concern for others.
- Increased independence and self-reliance.
- Peer relationships remain important.
- Development of more serious relationships.
- Social and cultural traditions regain some of their importance.

Adolescent Physical Development

During adolescence, young people go through many changes as they move into physical maturity. Early, prepubescent changes occur when the secondary sexual characteristics appear.

Girls may begin to develop breast buds as early as eight years old. Breasts develop fully between ages 12 - 18. Pubic hair, armpit and leg hair usually begin to grow at about age 9 - 10 and reach adult patterns at about 13 - 14 years. Menarche (the beginning of menstrual periods) typically occurs about two years after early breast and pubic hair appear. It may occur as early as age nine, or as late as age sixteen. The average age of menstruation in the United States is about twelve years. Girls growth spurt peaks around age 11.5 and slows around age sixteen.

Boys may begin to notice that their testicles and scrotum grow as early as age nine. Soon, the penis begins to lengthen. By age 17 - 18, their genitals are usually at their adult size and shape. Pubic hair growth, as well as armpit, leg, chest, and facial hair, begins in boys at about age twelve, and reaches adult patterns at about 17 - 18 years.

Boys do not start puberty with a sudden incident, like the beginning of menstrual periods in girls. Having regular nocturnal emissions (wet dreams) marks the beginning of puberty in boys. Wet dreams typically start between ages 13 - 17. The average age is about fourteen and a half years. Boys' voices change at the same time as the penis grows. Nocturnal emissions occur with the peak of the height spurt. Boys' growth spurt peaks around age thirteen and a half and slows around age eighteen.

Adolescent Behavior

The sudden and rapid physical changes that adolescents go through make adolescents very self-conscious. They are sensitive, and worried about their own body changes. They may make painful comparisons about themselves with their peers.

Physical changes may not occur in a smooth, regular schedule. Therefore, adolescents may go through awkward growth stages, both in their appearance and physical coordination. Girls may be anxious if they are not ready for the beginning of their menstrual periods. Boys may worry if they do not know about nocturnal emissions.

During adolescence, it is normal for young people to begin to separate from their parents and make their own identity. In some cases, this may occur without a problem from their parents and other family members. However, this may lead to conflict in some families as the parents try to keep control.

Friends become more important as adolescents pull away from their parents in a search for their own identity. Their peer group may become a safe haven. This allows the adolescent to test new ideas. In early adolescence, the peer group most often consists of non-romantic friendships. These often include cliques, gangs, or clubs. Members of the peer group often try to act alike, dress alike, have secret codes or rituals, and participate in the same activities.

As the youth moves into mid-adolescence (15 to 16 years) and beyond, the peer group expands to include romantic friendships. In mid- to late adolescence, young people often feel the need to establish their sexual identity. They need to become comfortable with their body and sexual feelings.

Adolescents learn to express and receive intimate or sexual advances. Young people who do not have the chance for such experiences may have a harder time with intimate relationships when they are adults. Adolescents very often have behaviors that are consistent with several myths of adolescence.

The first myth is that they are "on stage" and other people's attention is constantly centered on their appearance or actions.
This is normal self-centeredness. However, it may appear (especially to adults) to border on paranoia, self-love (narcissism), or even hysteria.

Another myth of adolescence is the idea that "it will never happen to me, only the other person." "It" may represent becoming pregnant or catching a sexually-transmitted disease after having unprotected sex, causing a car crash while driving under the influence of alcohol or drugs, or any of the many other negative effects of risk-taking behaviors.

Parenting Tips About Sexuality

Adolescents most often need privacy to understand the changes taking place in their bodies. Ideally, they should be allowed to have their own bedroom. If this is not possible, they should have at least some private space.

Teasing an adolescent child about physical changes is inappropriate. It may lead to self-consciousness and embarrassment. Parents need to remember that it is natural and normal for their adolescent to be interested in body changes and sexual topics. It does not mean that their child is involved in sexual activity.

Independence and Power Struggles

The teenager's quest to become independent is a normal part of development. The parent should not see it as a rejection or loss of control. Parents need to be constant and consistent. They should be available to listen to the child's ideas without dominating the child's independent identity.

Although adolescents always challenge authority figures, they need or want limits. Limits provide a safe boundary for them to grow and function. Limit-setting means having pre-set rules and regulations about their behavior.

Power struggles begin when authority is at stake or "being right" is the main issue. These situations should be avoided, if possible. One of the parties (typically the teen) will be overpowered. This will cause the youth to lose face. The adolescent may feel embarrassed, inadequate, resentful, and bitter as a result.

Parents should be ready for and recognize common conflicts that may develop while parenting adolescents. The experience may be affected by unresolved issues from the parent's own childhood, or from the adolescent's early years.

Parents should know that their adolescents will repeatedly challenge their authority. Keeping open lines of communication and clear, yet negotiable, limits or boundaries may help reduce major conflicts.

Most parents feel like they have more wisdom and self-growth as they rise to the challenges of parenting adolescents.

Key Points

- Adolescence is one of the most rapid phases of human development.

- Biological maturity precedes psychosocial maturity. This has implications for policy and program responses to the exploration and experimentation that takes place during adolescence.

- The characteristics of both the individual and the environment influence the changes taking place during adolescence.

- Younger adolescents may be particularly vulnerable when their mental capacities are still developing, and they are beginning to move outside the confines of their families.

- The changes in adolescence have health consequence not only in adolescence but also over the life-course.

- The unique nature and importance of adolescence mandates explicit and specific attention in health policy and programs.

Recognizing Adolescence

Adolescence is a period of life with specific health and developmental needs and rights. It is also a time to develop knowledge and skills, learn to manage emotions and relationships, and acquire attributes and abilities that will be important for enjoying the adolescent years and assuming adult roles.

All societies recognize that there is a difference between being a child and becoming an adult. How this transition from childhood to adulthood is defined and recognized differs between cultures and over time. In the past it has often been relatively rapid, and in some societies, it still is. In many countries, however, this is changing.

Age: Not the Whole Story

Age is a convenient way to define adolescence. But it is only one characteristic that delineates this period of development. Age is often more appropriate for assessing and comparing biological changes (e.g. puberty), which are fairly universal, than the social transitions, which vary more with the socio-cultural environment.

Adolescence: Physical Changes

Adolescence is one of the most rapid phases of human development. Although the order of many of the changes appears to be universal, their timing and the speed of change vary among and even within individuals. Both the characteristics of an individual (e.g. sex) and external factors (e.g. inadequate nutrition, an abusive environment) influence these changes.

Adolescence: Neurodevelopmental Changes

Important neuronal developments are also taking place during the adolescent years. These developments are linked to hormonal changes but are not always dependent on them. Developments are taking place in regions of the brain, such as the limbic system, that are responsible for pleasure seeking and reward processing, emotional responses and sleep regulation.

At the same time, changes are taking place in the pre-frontal cortex, the area responsible for what are called executive functions: decision-making, organization, impulse control and planning for the future. The changes in the pre-frontal cortex occur later in adolescence than the limbic system changes.

Adolescence: Psychological and Social Changes

Linked to the hormonal and neurodevelopmental changes that are taking place are psychosocial and emotional changes and increasing cognitive and intellectual capacities. Over the course of the second decade, adolescents develop stronger reasoning skills, logical and moral thinking, and become more capable of abstract thinking and making rational judgements.

Changes taking place in the adolescent's environment both affect and are affected by the internal changes of adolescence. These external influences, which differ among cultures and societies, include social values and norms and the changing roles, responsibilities, relationships and expectations of this period of life.

Implications for Health and Behavior

In many ways adolescent development drives the changes in the disease burden between childhood to adulthood, for example, the increase with age in sexual and reproductive health problems, mental illness and injuries.

The appearance of certain health problems in adolescence, including substance use disorders, mental disorders and injuries, likely reflects both the biological changes of puberty and the social context in which young people are growing up. Other conditions, such as the increased incidence of certain infectious diseases, for example, schistosomiasis, may simply result from the daily activities of adolescents during this period of their lives.

Many of the health-related behaviors that arise during adolescence have implications for both present and future health and development. For example, alcohol use and obesity in early adolescence not only compromise adolescent development, but they also predict health-compromising alcohol use and obesity in later life, with serious implications for public health.

15 – Risky Behavior and Teenage Pregnancy

Teenagers are bombarded with sexual content in music and the media. Parents need to talk with their teens about sex and make it clear to them from an early age to respect themselves and their bodies and should explain about the physical, emotional and social consequences of sexual promiscuity.

Teens don't always have access to reliable information, and parents should be the most reliable source for comprehensive information about sexuality and risk prevention. Promiscuity is a health risk, and your teen should know what the risks are, and the statistics.

The best way to halt the rates of teen pregnancy statistics from continuing to rise is to educate teens. It is important for parents to discuss sex and safe sex with their teens. It is also important for teens to pay attention and learn about teen sex and how to be safe about it.

The dangers of contracting sexually transmitted diseases (STDs) are very real, as is the risk of HIV and AIDS, cervical cancer and teenage pregnancies. Teenagers must be brought face to face with the threats of promiscuous sexual behavior. They must realize that promiscuity and any inappropriate sexual behavior can have a far-reaching impact on their lives.

Promiscuity is a teenage risky behavior problem that parents must address, however uncomfortable it may be to bring up the issues of sex with their teens. Promiscuity may be a warning sign that something is wrong, and parents need to be aware that risky behavior is often associated with other underlying problems. Promiscuity can be emotionally destructive and can lower your teen's self-esteem in the long term.

Even though the teen pregnancy rate has declined over the past few decades, the fact of the matter is that the United States has the highest teen pregnancy rate of the Western industrialized world. It is true that the teen pregnancy and birth rate was much higher prior to 1980 (and especially in the 1950s and 1960s), but at the time young women were getting married and having children before the age of twenty.

Most of the teen pregnancies occurring before 1980 were to married women; now most of today's teen mothers are unwed. This is a very disturbing statistic and a detriment to society in so many ways.

Risk Factors for Teen Pregnancy

There are certain risk factors that make some teens more likely to become pregnant than others. Educating yourself about those risk factors can help you take steps to mitigate the risks. Teens who experience any of the following may be at a higher risk of teenage pregnancy:

- Drug and alcohol use.
- Lack of knowledge about sex or contraception.
- Lack of goals for the future.
- Low self-esteem.
- Poor school performance.
- Having sex at a young age.

- Being the victim of sexual abuse.
- Negative attitude towards using contraception.
- Ambivalence about having a child.

Social Risk Factors

A teen's friends can play a big role in the decision to become sexually active. Here are some social risk factors to be on the lookout for:

- Pressure from peers to have sex.
- Dating at an early age.
- Dating older guys.
- Friends who are sexually active.
- Poor peer relationships.

Family Risk Factors

While you can't always control everything about your family, you can take steps to address some risk factors. Here are the risk factors that could put your teen at risk of teenage pregnancy:

- Poor parental supervision.
- Limited communication between parents and teen.
- Negative family interactions.
- Single-parent families.
- Significant unresolved conflict between family members.
- Family history of teenage pregnancies.

Preventing Teen Pregnancy

Even if you can't get rid of all the risk factors your teen may face, you can take steps to reduce the likelihood your teen will get pregnant. The most important thing you can do is talk to your teen about sex.

No matter whether your message is one of abstinence, and/or using contraceptives, delaying sex until the right time, talk about birth control. Make sure your teen has the facts about how to prevent an unplanned pregnancy.

Talk about your values and your expectations. If you make it clear that you disapprove of sex during high school, your teen may be less likely to become sexually active. But you should also make it clear that your teen can come to you with questions or concerns. The last thing you want is for your teen to hide things from you.

Hold open discussions and allow your teen to ask questions after the big talk(s). And most of all, help your teen become a well-rounded individual. Teens who have lots of interests, activities, and goals are less likely to become sexually active at an early age.

Teen Pregnancy Statistics

Between 1990 and 2006 we've seen visible decline in teen pregnancy rates and teen births, but it's still been estimated that three-in-ten girls in the United States get pregnant by the age of twenty. That's three-in-ten and let that sink for a moment! Think about your daughter and two of her friends and the probability that one of those three will be pregnant by the time they are twenty. Here are some more sobering teen pregnancy statistics:

- In 2013 273,105 babies were born to women ages 15 - 19.
- In 2013 there were 26.5 births for every 1,000 girls ages 15 - 19.
- 89% of teenage parents are unmarried.

- Over 86,000 teens aged 15 -17 gave birth in 2012.
- Nearly 1,700 teens aged 15 - 17 give birth every week.
- About 77% of teenage pregnancies are unplanned.
- Four-in-ten teenage girls who had sex at 13 - 14 report the sex was unwanted or involuntary.
- Fifteen percent of teen pregnancies end in miscarriage.
- 30% of teenage pregnancies end in abortion.

Teen Pregnancy by Ethnicity in 15 - 19-Year-Old Girls

When segmented into ethnicities, some of these pregnancy statistics become even more alarming. For example, both black and Hispanic girls show a pregnancy rate before the age of twenty over 50%. That is every other girl! It gets no better in the following years as six-in-ten pregnancies to women aged 20 - 24 were unplanned.

- 41.7 per 1,000 Hispanic girls reported a teen pregnancy in 2013.
- 39.0 per 1,000 black girls reported a teen pregnancy in 2013.
- 18.6 per 1,000 white girls reported a teen pregnancy in 2013.
- 9.0 per 1,000 Asian girls reported a teen pregnancy in 2013.

Even though over all teen pregnancy rate in the United States are falling, the fact remains that the U.S. remains in the lead as far as teen pregnancy in the industrialized world is concerned. What puts teenagers in the U.S. more at risk for teen pregnancy? The answer to risk factors for teen pregnancy involve a variety of complex and intertwined reasons related to early and unsafe sexual activity.

Teens Becoming Sexually Active Earlier

One of the influences on the risk of a teen to become pregnant includes how early that teen becomes sexually active. More teens are becoming sexually active at younger ages. It is especially worth noting that teen pregnancy rates among girls under the age of fifteen are on the rise, rather than in decline.

Nonetheless, these teens are more likely to go on to have more intercourse and, as a result, more likely to have a teen pregnancy. For high school students reporting in 2009 that they had ever had sexual intercourse, percentages were highest among black males (72%) and females (58%), followed by Hispanic males (53%) and females (45%), and white females (45%) and males (40%), and Asian females (24%) and males (20%).

Attitudes About Birth Control

Teens who do not use birth control are obviously at higher risk for teen pregnancy. Many teenagers find it difficult obtain birth control, and others are embarrassed to use it. This is especially true of condoms. Teens who do not have the dexterity or practice with condoms are more likely to use them improperly and/or avoid using them, and therefore become involved in creating a teen pregnancy.

Cultural differences also play a part. Hispanics are the least likely to use birth control, followed by blacks. This contributes to the teen pregnancy statistic that Hispanics, followed by blacks, have the highest rates of teen pregnancy.

Socioeconomic Factors in Teen Pregnancy Risk

The socioeconomic status of a teenager's family can present further risk of teen pregnancy. Risky sexual behaviors in teens are more likely to occur in poor families, and among those with single parents. Indeed, a study found that teens girls whose fathers were not present in the home were more likely to become pregnant than those who had regular contact and good relationships with their fathers.

Parents' educational level also contributed to the risk of teen pregnancy. Those teenagers whose parents have lower levels of education are more likely to engage in risky sexual behavior, and more likely to become pregnant.

Teen Religious and Educational Involvement

Teenagers who have a low involvement in religious and educational activities are more likely to experience teen pregnancy. Involvement in religious activities is one of the strongest factors related to a later sexual debut (including waiting until marriage). Additionally, teens that focus on school activity are less likely to engage in intercourse and are more likely to use birth control when they do.

The Reasons Teens Get Pregnant

There are many reasons that teenagers become pregnant. Some of them want to have babies. However, the fact of the matter is that most teen pregnancies are unintentional (80%). Additionally, most of them occur to unwed teen mothers. This means that even though most teens do not want to become pregnant, they are still becoming so as a result of sexual activity. While actual force to have sex is rare, many teenage girls (especially those under the age of 15) feel pressured to have sex. And, of course, the more intercourse a teenager has, the more likely it is that a teen pregnancy will eventually result.

Unwanted Sexual Intercourse

Rape does happen and is one of the reasons that teen pregnancies occur. Date rape by boyfriends, family members and even strangers can result in teen pregnancy. However, many teenagers feel pressure of a subtler kind.

Most teenage girls who engage in sexual activity, and especially those who do so before the age of fifteen, admit that they wish they had waited. But often they feel pressure from their boyfriends: three out of four girls report that the reason they have sex is because their boyfriends want them to. Most of these teens regret it later, whether they become pregnant.

Inconsistent Use of Birth Control

Even though the use of contraceptives has increased among teenagers, its use remains spotty. Teens may use birth control to help prevent teen pregnancy, but most do not use contraceptives consistently. Erratic contraceptive use, however, is better than none.

A sexually active teen that does not use any birth control has a 90% chance of becoming pregnant within a year. Some of the reasons that birth control is not used include the following: uneducated about birth control, uncomfortable using birth control methods and unable to access reliable birth control.

Researchers and administrative members of family-planning services throughout the United States attribute a lack of access to birth control as one of the most common reasons for these unplanned pregnancies. Many women and teens are living in a state of denial thinking that they will get lucky and won't get pregnant.

However, this is not the case. About 80% of women and teens that don't use contraception or birth control will get pregnant within a year. This high statistic is what leads so many women and teens to experience an unplanned pregnancy.

Teenage Abortion Statistics

Unfortunately, about 25% of these unintended pregnancies are unwanted and often result in abortion or adoption. About 27% of all teenage pregnancies result in abortion.

Teenage abortion statistics are strongly linked to teen pregnancy rates, and the numbers for both have declined from their peak in the 1980s. The numbers in the US are still high compared to most other developed nations and the negative physical, emotional, and social consequences that pregnancy and abortion can have on a teen's life is alarming.

Though many abortions occur because teens are facing an unwanted pregnancy, which is known as elective abortion. Abortions are also performed in cases of rape or incest, when the pregnancy is threatening the health of the mother or the fetus is not viable.

These numbers of unintended pregnancies are more likely to occur to teens and women of lower incomes that do not have the money or resources to pay for birth control. These women also might not have access to pregnancy prevention education and don't know or understand what options they have when it comes to protecting themselves during sex.

Some unplanned pregnancy statistics show that about 48% of women who have had unplanned births were using a contraceptive during the month they became pregnant. Unfortunately, many teens that use condoms have been shown to not do so consistently, although condom use among teens is up.

Others that use the birth control pill are not as diligent about taking the pill regularly, thereby decreasing the effectiveness of the birth control pill, which can result in cases of pregnancy.

Contraceptive Use

The proportion of U.S. females aged 15 - 19 who used contraceptives the first time they had sex has increased, from 48% in 1982 to 79% in 2011–2013. Adolescents who report having had sex at age fourteen or younger are less likely than those who initiated sex later to have used a contraceptive method at first sex.

The condom is the contraceptive method most commonly used at first intercourse. In 2006–2010, 68% of females and 80% of males aged 15 - 19 reported having used a condom the first time they had sex. In 2006–2010, 86% of females and 93% of males aged 15 - 19 reported having used contraceptives the last time they had sex.

These proportions represent a marked increase since 1995, when 71% of females and 82% of males in that age-group reported use of a contraceptive method at last sex. However, the proportions were generally unchanged between 2002 and 2006–2010. In 2012, four-percent of female contraceptive users aged 15 - 19 used a long-acting reversible contraceptive method (IUD or implant) in the last month.

Dual method uses (i.e., use of a condom in combination with a short- or long-term reversible contraceptive method) can offer protection against both pregnancy and STIs. In 2006–2010, one in five sexually active females aged 15 - 19 and one-third of sexually active males in this age-group said that they used both a condom and a hormonal method the last time they had sex. In 2006–2010, fourteen percent of sexually experienced females aged 15 - 19 had ever used emergency contraception.

Adolescents in the United States and Europe have similar levels of sexual activity. However, European adolescents are more likely than U.S. adolescents to use contraceptives and to use the most effective methods; they also have substantially lower pregnancy rates.

Access to and Use of Contraceptive Services

Current federal law requires health insurance plans to cover the full range of female contraceptive methods, including counseling and related services, without out-of-pocket costs. However, some minors may not use insurance to access contraceptive services because they are not aware that these services are covered or because of confidentiality concerns.

No state explicitly requires parental consent or notification for minors to obtain contraceptive services. However, two states (Texas and Utah) require parental consent for contraceptive services paid for with state funds.

A Father's Rulebook on the Do's and Don'ts for Dating His Little Princess

Twenty-one states and the District of Columbia explicitly allow minors to obtain contraceptive services without a parent's involvement. Another 25 states have affirmed that right for certain classes of minors, while four states do not have a statute or policy on the subject. The U.S. Supreme Court has ruled that minors' privacy rights include the right to obtain contraceptive services.

Even when parental consent is not required for contraceptive services, concerns about confidentiality may limit adolescents' access to or use of contraceptive or other reproductive health services. In 2013–2015, eighteen percent of 15 - 17-year-olds and seven percent of 18 - 19-year-olds reported that they would not seek sexual or reproductive health care because of concerns that their parents might find out.

In 2006–2010, 66% of sexually active females aged 15 - 19 reported having received contraceptive services in the last year; about one-third had received this care from publicly funded clinics and the rest from private health care providers.

In 2014, an estimated 4.7 million women younger than twenty were in need of publicly funded contraceptive care because they were sexually active and neither pregnant nor trying to become pregnant.

Nearly one million 15 - 19-year-old women in need of publicly funded contraceptive services received them from publicly supported family planning centers in 2014. These services helped adolescents to avert 232,000 unintended pregnancies, 118,000 unplanned births and 76,000 abortions.

While school-based health centers are an important source of sexual and reproductive health services for students across the United States, only 37% of these centers dispensed contraceptives in 2010–2011. Many are prohibited from doing so by state or local policies.

16 – Sexually Transmitted Diseases and Infections

In the United States there were roughly nineteen million new cases of sexually transmitted infections in 2010. Sexually transmitted infections (STI), also referred to as sexually transmitted diseases (STD) and venereal diseases (VD), are infections that are commonly spread by sex, especially vaginal intercourse, anal sex or oral sex. Throughout this book, both STD and STI terms are used interchangeably.

Adolescents are disproportionately affected by sexually transmitted infections (STIs). Young people ages 15 - 24 represent 25% of the sexually active population, but acquire half of all new STIs, which amounts to 9.8 million new cases a year. About 3.2 million adolescent females are infected with at least one of the most common STIs. Today, two in five sexually active teen girls have had an STD that can cause infertility and even death. In 2011, approximately 24% of new HIV diagnoses were young people between the ages of 13 - 24.

More than 30 different bacteria, viruses, and parasites can be transmitted through sexual activity. Bacterial STIs include chlamydia, gonorrhea, and syphilis among others. Viral STIs include genital herpes, HIV/AIDS, genital warts, and parasitic STIs include trichomoniasis.

Human papillomavirus is the most common STI among teens; some estimates find that up to 35% of teens ages 14 - 19 have HPV. Girls age 15 - 19 have the highest rates of Gonorrhea and the second highest rate of Chlamydia of any age group.

The most effective way to prevent STIs and STDs is to abstain from sexual activity and if teens are having sex, they should be using a condom correctly and with every sexual act. Safer sex practices such as use of condoms, having a smaller number of sexual partners, and being in a relationship where each person only has sex with the other also decreases the risk.

The Various Types of STIs and the Transmission Mechanisms

If you're like me, when I first put this list together I was shocked regarding how many STDs and STIs are out there and how prevalent they are. Even if you take into consideration using contraceptives and using them properly, the odds nonetheless, of contracting and or spreading one of these is sobering and frightening. Choosing to have sex with anyone who might have contracted one of these is taking a big gamble and risk.

Bacterial

- Chancroid (Haemophilus ducreyi).
- Chlamydia (Chlamydia trachomatis).
- Gonorrhea (Neisseria gonorrhoeae), colloquially known as "the clap."
- Granuloma inguinale or (Klebsiella granulomatis).
- Mycoplasma genitalium.
- Mycoplasma hominis.
- Syphilis (Treponema pallidum).

- Ureaplasma infection.

Fungal

- Candidiasis (yeast infection).

Viral

- Viral hepatitis (Hepatitis B virus), saliva, venereal fluids. (Note: Hepatitis A and Hepatitis E are transmitted via the fecal-oral route; Hepatitis C is rarely sexually transmittable, and the route of transmission of Hepatitis D (only if infected with B) is uncertain but may include sexual transmission).

- Herpes simplex (Herpes simplex virus 1, 2) skin and mucosal, transmissible with or without visible blisters.

- HIV (Human Immunodeficiency Virus), venereal fluids, semen, breast milk, blood.

- HPV (Human Papillomavirus), skin and mucosal contact. 'High risk' types of HPV cause almost all cervical cancers, as well as some anal, penile, and vulvar cancer. Some other types of HPV cause genital warts.

- Molluscum contagiosum (molluscum contagiosum virus MCV), close contact.

Parasites

- Crab louse, colloquially known as "crabs" or "pubic lice" (Pthirus pubis). The infestation and accompanying inflammation is Pediculosis pubis.

- Scabies (Sarcoptes scabiei).

Protozoal

- Trichomoniasis (Trichomonas vaginalis), colloquially known as "trich."

Sexually Transmitted Infections Include These Symptoms

As noted previously, the list of how many STDs and STIs are out there and how prevalent they are is shocking. Even if you take into consideration using contraceptives and using them properly, the odds nonetheless, of contracting and or spreading one of these is sobering and frightening. It almost reminds me of Russian roulette and those kind of odds and chances of contracting one of these are not the ones I would want for my daughter. Or yours either!

Chlamydia

Chlamydia is a sexually transmitted infection caused by the bacterium Chlamydia trachomatis. In women, symptoms may include abnormal vaginal discharge, burning during urination, and bleeding in between periods, although most women do not experience any symptoms. Symptoms in men include pain when urinating, and abnormal discharge from their penis.

If left untreated in both men and women, Chlamydia can infect the urinary tract and potentially lead to pelvic inflammatory disease (PID). PID can cause serious problems during pregnancy and even has the potential to cause infertility. It can cause a woman to have a potentially deadly ectopic pregnancy, in which the egg implants outside of the uterus. However, Chlamydia can be cured with antibiotics.

Herpes (HSV-1 and HSV-2)

The two most common forms of herpes are caused by infection with herpes simplex virus (HSV). HSV-1 is typically acquired orally and causes cold sores, HSV-2 is usually acquired during sexual contact and affects the genitals, however either strain may affect either site.

Some people are asymptomatic or have very mild symptoms. Those that do experience symptoms usually notice them two to twenty days after exposure which last two to four weeks. Symptoms can include small fluid-filled blisters, headaches, backaches, itching or tingling sensations in the genital or anal area, pain during urination, Flu like symptoms, swollen glands, or fever.

Herpes is spread through skin contact with a person infected with the virus. The virus affects the areas where it entered the body. This can occur through kissing, vaginal intercourse, oral sex or anal sex. The virus is most infectious during times when there are visible symptoms, however those who are asymptomatic can still spread the virus through skin contact.

The initial infection and symptoms are usually the most severe because the body does not have any antibodies built up. After the primary attack, one might have recurring attacks that are milder or might not even have future attacks.

There is no cure for the disease but there are antiviral medications that treat its symptoms and lower the risk of transmission (Valtrex). Although HSV-1 is typically the "oral" version of the virus, and HSV-2 is typically the "genital" version of the virus, a person with HSV-1 orally CAN transmit that virus to their partner genitally.

The virus, either type, will settle into a nerve bundle either at the top of the spine, producing the "oral" outbreak, or a second nerve bundle at the base of the spine, producing the genital outbreak.

Human Papillomavirus (HPV)

The human papillomavirus (HPV) is the most common STI in the United States. There are more than 40 different strains of HPV and many do not cause any health problems. In 90% of cases the body's immune system clears the infection naturally within two years.

Some cases may not be cleared and can lead to genital warts (bumps around the genitals that can be small or large, raised or flat, or shaped like cauliflower) or cervical cancer and other HPV related cancers. Symptoms might not show up until advanced stages.

It is important for women to get pap smears to check for and treat cancers. There are also two vaccines available for women (Cervarix and Gardasil) that protect against the types of HPV that cause cervical cancer. HPV can be passed through genital-to-genital contact as well as during oral sex. It is important to remember that the infected partner might not have any symptoms.

Gonorrhea

Gonorrhea is caused by bacterium that lives on moist mucous membranes in the urethra, vagina, rectum, mouth, throat, and eyes. The infection can spread through contact with the penis, vagina, mouth or anus. Symptoms of gonorrhea usually appear two to five days after contact with an infected partner however, some men might not notice symptoms for up to a month.

Symptoms in men include burning and pain while urinating, increased urinary frequency, discharge from the penis (white, green, or yellow in color), red or swollen urethra, swollen or tender testicles, or sore throat.

Symptoms in women may include vaginal discharge, burning or itching while urinating, painful sexual intercourse, severe pain in lower abdomen (if infection spreads to fallopian tubes), or fever (if infection spreads to fallopian tubes); however, many women do not show any symptoms. There are some antibiotic resistant strains for Gonorrhea, but most cases can be cured with antibiotics.

Syphilis

Syphilis is an STI caused by a bacterium. Untreated, it can lead to complications and death. Clinical manifestations of syphilis include the ulceration of the uro-genital tract, mouth or rectum; if left untreated the symptoms worsen.

In recent years, the prevalence of syphilis has declined in Western Europe, but it has increased in Eastern Europe (former Soviet states). A high incidence of syphilis can be found in places such as

Cameroon, Cambodia, Papua New Guinea. Syphilis infections are increasing in the United States.

Trichomoniasis

Trichomoniasis is a common STI that is caused by infection with a protozoan parasite called Trichomonas vaginalis. Trichomoniasis affects both women and men, but symptoms are more common in women. Most patients are treated with an antibiotic called metronidazole, which is very effective.

Human Immunodeficiency Virus (HIV)

HIV (human immunodeficiency virus) damages the body's immune system, which interferes with its ability to fight off disease-causing agents. The virus kills CD4 cells, which are white blood cells that help fight off various infections. HIV is carried in body fluids and is spread by sexual activity.

It can also be spread by contact with infected blood, breast feeding, childbirth, and from mother to child during pregnancy. When HIV is at its most advanced stage, an individual is said to have AIDS (acquired immunodeficiency syndrome). There are different stages of the progression of and HIV infection. The stages include primary infection, asymptomatic infection, symptomatic infection, and AIDS.

In the primary infection stage, an individual will have flu like symptoms (headache, fatigue, fever, muscle aches) for about two weeks. In the asymptomatic stage, symptoms usually disappear, and the patient can remain asymptomatic for years. When HIV progresses to the symptomatic stage, the immune system is weakened, and has a low cell count of CD4+ T Cells. When the HIV infection becomes life-threatening, it is called AIDS.

People with AIDS fall prey to opportunistic infections and die as a result. When the disease was first discovered in the 1980s, those who had AIDS were not likely to live longer than a few years. There are now antiretroviral drugs (ARVs) available to treat HIV infections. There is no known cure for HIV or AIDS, but the drugs help suppress the virus. By suppressing the amount of virus in the body, people can lead longer and healthier lives. Even though their virus levels may be low they can still spread the virus to others.

Screening for STIs and STDs

Specific age groups, persons who participate in risky sexual behavior, or those have certain health conditions may require screening for STIs. The CDC recommends that sexually active women under the age of 25 and those over 25 at risk should be screened for chlamydia and gonorrhea yearly.

Appropriate times for screening are during regular pelvic examinations and preconception evaluations. Nucleic acid amplification tests are the recommended method of diagnosis for gonorrhea and chlamydia. This can be done on urine in both men and women, vaginal or cervical swabs in women, or urethral swabs in men.

Early identification and treatment results in less chance to spread disease, and for some conditions may improve the outcomes of treatment. There is often a window period after initial infection during which an STI test will be negative. During this period, the infection may be transmissible. The duration of this period varies depending on the infection and the test. Diagnosis may also be delayed by reluctance of the infected person to seek a medical professional. One report indicated that people turn to the internet rather than to a medical professional for information on STIs to a higher degree than for other sexual problems.

Group Disparities in Acquiring and Spreading STIs and STDs

Health disparities and various differences in the incidence, prevalence, and mortality of a disease and the related adverse health conditions exist among specific population groups.

These groups may be characterized by gender, age, race or ethnicity, education, income, social class, disability, geographic location, or sexual orientation. These health disparities are one reason why HIV/AIDS, viral hepatitis, STDs, and TB take a greater toll in one population group over another.

HIV/AIDS

In 2014, the estimated diagnosis rate for HIV cases in the United States was 13.8 per 100,000 population and 49.4 among blacks. Of 222,185 estimated diagnoses of HIV infection in the United States and six dependent areas from 2010 to 2014, blacks accounted for the following:

- 45% of the total.
- 62% of women.
- 64% of infections attributed to heterosexual contact.
- 64% of children of all ages.

In 2013, the death rate for blacks was higher (19.4 per 100,000) compared with any other racial ethnicity group (2.5 whites). In 2013, blacks represented 47% of all estimated deaths of people ever diagnosed with HIV. (Note that deaths could be from any cause). A recent study showed that blacks diagnosed with HIV are less likely than other groups to be linked to care, retained in care, receive antiretroviral treatment and achieve adequate viral suppression.

Black men accounted for 40% of HIV cases diagnosed among men in the United States and six dependent areas in 2014. A majority (78%) of black men diagnosed with HIV contracted the disease through male-to-male sexual contact while fifteen percent contracted HIV through heterosexual exposure.

Among black women in the United States and six dependent areas, heterosexual contact was the most frequently cited mode of transmission, accounting for 91% of cases diagnosed in 2014.

In 2014, Hispanics made up seventeen percent of the population of the United States but accounted for 23% of estimated diagnoses of HIV infection.

In 2014, Asians made up five percent of the American population and accounted for two percent of HIV infection diagnoses. Asian American rates of HIV infection are very low compared to other racial/ethnic groups.

Gonorrhea

In 2014, 55.4% of all reported cases of gonorrhea occurred among blacks. The rate of gonorrhea among blacks in 2014 was 405.4 cases per 100,000 population, which was 10.6 times the rate among whites (38.3). This disparity has changed little in recent years. This disparity was similar for black men (10.6 times) and black women (10.7 times).

In 2014, the gonorrhea rate among Hispanics was 73.3 cases per 100,000 population, which was 1.9 times the rate among whites. This disparity was similar for Hispanic women (1.8 times the rate among white women) and Hispanic men (2.0 times the rate among white men).

In 2014, the gonorrhea rate among Asians was 19.3 cases per 100,000 population, which was lower than (0.5 times) the rate among whites. This difference is larger for Asian women than for Asian men.

Chlamydia

In 2014, the overall rate among blacks in the United States was 1,117.9 cases per 100,000, a 6.2% decrease from the 2010 rate of 1,167 cases per 100,000. The rate of chlamydia among black women was 5.7 times the rate among white women (1,432 and 253 per 100,000 women, respectively). The chlamydia rate among black men was 7.3 times the rate among white men (772 and 105 cases per 100,000 men, respectively).

In 2014, the chlamydia rate among Hispanics was 380 cases per 100,000 population, which is an increase from the 2013 rate of 377 cases per 100,000 and 2.1 times the rate among whites.

In 2014, the chlamydia rate among Asians was 112 cases per 100,000 population, an increase from the 2013 rate of 111 cases per 100,000. The overall rate among Asians was lower than the rate among whites.

Syphilis

During 2010–2014, the rate of primary and secondary (P&S) syphilis among blacks increased 7.8% (from 17.8 to 119 cases per 100,000 population). In 2014, 38% of all cases reported to CDC were among blacks.

The overall 2014 rate for blacks was 5.4 times the rate for whites, while the 2013 rate was 5.6 times the rate for whites. In 2014, the rate of P&S syphilis among black men was 5.3 times the rate among white men; the rate among black women was 9.2 times the rate among white women.

In 2014, the rate of congenital syphilis was 38.2 cases per 100,000 live births among blacks. Race/ethnicity for cases of congenital syphilis is based on the mother's race/ethnicity. This rate was 10.3 times the rate among whites (3.7 cases per 100,000 live births).

In 2014, the rate of primary and secondary (P&S) syphilis among Hispanics was 7.6 cases per 100,000 population. The 2014 rate of P&S syphilis for Hispanics was 2.2 times the rate for whites. This disparity was similar for Hispanic women (2.2 times the rate among white women) and Hispanic men (2.1 times the rate among white men).

In 2014, the rate of congenital syphilis was 12.1 cases per 100,000 live births among Hispanics. Race/ethnicity for cases of congenital syphilis is based on the mother's race/ethnicity. This rate was 3.3 times the rate among whites (3.7 cases per 100,000 live births).

In 2014, the rate of primary and secondary (P&S) syphilis among Asians was 2.8 cases per 100,000 population. The 2014 rate of P&S syphilis for Asians was 0.8 times the rate for whites. This difference is larger for Asian women (0.4 times the rate among white women) than for Asian men (0.9 times the rate among white men).

Acute Hepatitis A

During the past five years, there has been little difference between the rates of acute hepatitis A among whites and blacks. The 2014 rates for these groups were 0.28 and 0.20 cases per 100,000 population, respectively.

In 2014, the rate of hepatitis A among Hispanics was 0.38 cases per 100,000 population, the lowest rate recorded for this group.

Although rates of acute hepatitis A among Asian/Pacific Islanders have continued to decline, this group has had the highest rate since 2008. In 2014 the rate of hepatitis A for Asian/Pacific Islanders was 0.73 per 100,000 population in 2014.

Acute Hepatitis B

In 2014, the rate of acute hepatitis B was highest for blacks (0.88 cases per 100,000 population).

In 2014, the rate of acute hepatitis B was lowest for Hispanics and Asian/Pacific Islanders (0.29 cases per 100,000 population for each group).

In 2014, the rate of acute hepatitis B was lowest for Asian/Pacific Islanders and Hispanics (0.29 cases per 100,000 population for each group. However, regarding Chronic Hepatitis B, in 2014, among the 1784 cases for whom race/ethnicity was known, Asian/Pacific Islanders accounted for the highest number of chronic HBV cases (60%) reported from all seven funded sites.

Acute Hepatitis C

During 2002–2011, the incidence rate of acute hepatitis C remained below 0.5 cases per 100,000. The rate increased to 0.6 cases per 100,000 population in 2012 and to 0.7 cases per 100,000 population in 2013 and 2014. The rate of hepatitis C among blacks decreased five percent between 2013 and 2014 (from 0.2 cases per 100,000 in 2013 to 0.19 case per 100,000 population in 2014).

During 2002–2011, the incidence rate of acute hepatitis C remained below 0.5 cases per 100,000. The rate increased to 0.6 cases per 100,000 population in 2012 and to 0.7 cases per 100,000 population in 2013 and 2014. The rate of hepatitis C among Hispanics increased 13.6% (from 0.22 cases per 100,000 population in 2013 to 0.25 case per 100,000 population in 2014).

Rates for acute hepatitis C decreased for all racial/ethnic populations through 2003. During 2002–2011, the incidence rate of acute hepatitis C remained below 0.5 cases per 100,000. The rate increased to 0.6 cases per 100,000 population in 2012 and to 0.7 cases per 100,000 population in 2013 and 2014. In 2014 Asian/Pacific Islanders had the lowest rate for hepatitis C at 0.07 case per 100,000 population.

Prevention

The Centers for Disease Control and Prevention strategies for reducing STD risk include: vaccination, mutual monogamy, reducing the number of sexual partners and abstinence.

The most effective way to prevent sexual transmission of STIs is to avoid contact of body parts or fluids which can lead to transfer with an infected partner. Not all sexual activities involve contact: cybersex, phone sex or masturbation from a distance are methods of avoiding contact. Proper use of condoms reduces contact and risk. Although a condom is effective in limiting exposure, some disease transmission may occur even with a condom.

Both partners can get tested for STIs before initiating sexual contact, or before resuming contact if a partner engaged in contact with someone else. Many infections are not detectable immediately after exposure, so enough time must be allowed between possible exposures and testing for the tests to be accurate. Certain STIs, particularly certain persistent viruses like HPV, may be impossible to detect with current medical procedures.

Some treatment facilities utilize in-home test kits and have the person return the test for follow-up. Other facilities strongly encourage that those previously infected return to ensure that the infection has been eliminated. Novel strategies to foster re-testing have been the use of text messaging and email as reminders. These types of reminders are now used in addition to phone calls and letters.

After obtaining a sexual history, a healthcare provider can encourage risk reduction by providing prevention counseling. Prevention counseling is most effective if provided in a nonjudgmental and empathetic manner appropriate to the person's culture, language, gender, sexual orientation, age, and developmental level.

Vaccines

Vaccines are available that protect against some viral STIs, such as Hepatitis A, Hepatitis B, and some types of HPV. Vaccination before initiation of sexual contact is advised to assure maximal protection. The development of vaccines to protect against gonorrhea is ongoing.

Condoms

Condoms and female condoms only provide protection when used properly as a barrier, and only to and from the area that they cover. Uncovered areas are still susceptible to many STIs.

In the case of HIV, sexual transmission routes almost always involve the penis, as HIV cannot spread through unbroken skin; therefore, properly shielding the penis with a properly worn condom from the vagina or anus effectively stops HIV transmission. An infected fluid to broken skin born from a direct transmission of HIV would not be considered "sexually transmitted," but can still theoretically occur during sexual contact. This can be avoided simply by not engaging in sexual contact when presenting open, bleeding wounds.

Other STIs, even viral infections, can be prevented with the use of latex, polyurethane or polyisoprene condoms as a barrier. Some microorganisms and viruses are small enough to pass through the pores in natural skin condoms but are still too large to pass through latex or synthetic condoms.

A Father's Rulebook on the Do's and Don'ts for Dating His Little Princess

17 – Teen Dating Violence and Unhealthy Relationships

Teen dating violence (TDV) is defined as the physical, sexual, psychological, or emotional violence within a dating relationship, including stalking. It can occur in person or electronically and might occur between a current or former dating partner. Several different words and terms are used to describe teen dating violence. Below are just a few.

- Relationship abuse.

- Intimate partner violence.

- Relationship violence.

- Dating abuse.

- Domestic abuse.

- Domestic violence.

Warning Signs of Dating Violence

Dating violence is widespread with serious long-term and short-term effects. Many teens do not report it because they are afraid to tell friends and family. A 2017 CDC Report found that approximately seven percent of women and four percent of men who ever experienced rape, physical violence, or stalking by an intimate partner first experienced some form of partner violence by that partner before eighteen years of age.

- ➢ Your dating partner is using threats or violence to solve a problem.

- ➢ Frequent calling and texting to check where you are or who you are with or other jealous behavior.

- ➢ Telling you who you can spend time with, what you can do, or what to wear.

- ➢ Name calling, putting you down, embarrassing you, or making you feel bad about yourself.

- ➢ Making threats towards you, your family, and your friends.

- ➢ Making threats of suicide or self-harm.

- ➢ Forcing you to do something you don't want to do.

How Does Teen Dating Violence Differ from Adult Intimate Partner Violence?

An article published by the National Institute of Justice discusses current research on TDV and concludes that there are three key differences between adult and teen dating relationships.

Abusive teen relationships typically lack the same unequal power dynamic found in adult intimate partner violence relationships. Adolescent girls are not often dependent on their partner for financial support and do not typically have children to provide for and protect.

Teens have limited experience with romantic relationships and negotiating conflict and are more readily affected by the influence of peers. Because the dynamics of intimate partner abuse are different in adolescent and adult relationships, it is important not to apply an adult framework of intimate partner violence to teen dating violence.

Ten Facts About Teen Dating Violence

The 2013 national Youth Risk Behavior Survey found approximately ten percent of high school students reported physical victimization and ten percent reported sexual victimization from a dating partner in the twelve months before they were surveyed. They also discovered that:

- Each year approximately one in four adolescents report some form of verbal, physical, emotional or sexual abuse.

- Approximately one in five adolescents report being a victim of emotional abuse.

- Approximately one in five high school girls has been physically or sexually abused by a dating partner.

- Dating violence among their peers is reported by 54% of high school students.

- One in three teens report knowing a friend or peer who has been physically hurt by his or her partner through violent actions which included hitting, punching, kicking, slapping, and/or choking.

- Eighty percent of teens believe verbal abuse is a serious issue for their age group.

- Nearly 80% of girls who have been victims of physical abuse in their dating relationships continue to date the abuser.

- Nearly twenty percent of teen girls who have been in a relationship said that their boyfriend had threatened violence or self-harm in the event of a break-up.

- Nearly 70% of young women who have been raped knew their rapist; the perpetrator was or had been a boyfriend, friend, or casual acquaintance.

- The majority of teen dating abuse occurs in the home of one of the partners.

Problematic Behaviors

Are you going out with someone who displays any of the following concerning tendencies?

- Is jealous and possessive, won't let you have friends, checks up on you, won't accept breaking up.

- Tries to control you by being bossy, giving orders, making all the decisions, not taking your opinions seriously.

- Puts you down in front of friends or tells you that you would be nothing without him or her.

- Scares you? Makes you worry about reactions to things you say or do? Threatens you? Uses or owns weapons.

- Is violent? Has a history of fighting, loses temper quickly, brags about mistreating others? Grabs, pushes, shoves, or hits you.

- Pressures you for sex or is forceful or scary about sex? Gets too serious about the relationship too fast.

- Abuses alcohol or other drugs and pressures you to take them.

- Has a history of failed relationships and blames the other person for all of their problems.

- Makes your family and friends feel uneasy and concerned for your safety.

What Are the Consequences of Dating Violence?

As teens develop emotionally, they are heavily influenced by experiences in their relationships. Healthy relationship behaviors can have a positive effect on a teen's emotional development. Unhealthy, abusive, or violent relationships can have severe consequences and short- and long-term negative effects on a developing teen. Youth who experience dating violence are more likely to experience the following:

- Symptoms of depression and anxiety.
- Engagement in unhealthy behaviors, such as tobacco and drug use, and alcohol.
- Involvement in antisocial behaviors.
- Thoughts about suicide.
- Additionally, youth who are victims of dating violence in high school are at higher risk for victimization during college.

Why Does Dating Violence Happen?

Communicating with your partner, managing uncomfortable emotions like anger and jealousy, and treating others with respect are a few ways to keep relationships healthy and nonviolent. Teens receive messages about how to behave in relationships from peers, adults in their lives, and the media. All too often these examples suggest that violence in a relationship is normal.

As adults we know better, because any type of violence is never acceptable. There are reasons why violence occurs and is related to certain risk factors. Risks of having unhealthy relationships increase for teens who:

- Believe that dating violence is acceptable.
- Are depressed, anxious, or have other symptoms of trauma.

- Display aggression towards peers or display other aggressive behaviors.
- Use drugs or illegal substances.
- Engage in early sexual activity and have multiple sexual partners.
- Have a friend involved in dating violence.
- Have conflicts with a partner.
- Witness or experience violence in the home.

Dating violence is a type of intimate partner violence. It occurs between two people in a close relationship. The nature of dating violence can be physical, emotional, or sexual.

- Physical, this occurs when a partner is pinched, hit, shoved, slapped, punched, or kicked.
- Psychological/Emotional, this means threatening a partner or harming his or her sense of self-worth. Examples include name calling, shaming, bullying, embarrassing on purpose, or keeping him or her away from friends and family.
- Sexual, this is forcing a partner to engage in a sex act when he or she does not or cannot consent. This can be physical or nonphysical, like threatening to spread rumors if a partner refuses to have sex.
- Stalking, this refers to a pattern of harassing or threatening tactics that are unwanted and cause fear in the victim.

Dating violence can take place in person or electronically, such as repeated texting or posting sexual pictures of a partner online.

Unhealthy relationships can start early and last a lifetime. Teens often think some behaviors, like teasing and name calling, are a "normal" part of a relationship. However, these behaviors can become abusive and develop into more serious forms of violence.

Teen Dating Violence: What Parents and Teens Should Know

Dating violence doesn't just come in the form of physical abuse; it can also be emotional, psychological or sexual. Anyone can be affected, regardless of gender, race, religion, sexual orientation or socioeconomic status. Sadly, many teens who are the victims of teen dating violence suffer in silence.

Research finds only one-third of these youth ever tell someone about the abuse. Whether they are ashamed, afraid or struggling with guilt, many teens who experience dating violence keep the brutal secret hidden from the very people who could help most, their parents. Sadly, according to a study in the Journal of Adolescent Health, most parents, 65.5% reported they never spoke with their child about teen dating violence.

It's important that teens and parents talk about teen dating violence. But as a parent, would you know if your teen was in an abusive relationship? According to research conducted by Teen Research Unlimited, many parents are unable to detect the signs of dating abuse.

In a survey, 82% of parents reported feeling confident in their ability to recognize abuse signs, but only 42% could accurately identify signs of abuse. With one-in-three teens experiencing physical, sexual or emotional dating abuse, it's important that teens know the characteristics of an abusive relationship and that parents know how to proactively protect their teens.

For Teens: Be Alert to Signs of an Abusive Relationship

Do any of the following unhealthy relationship characteristics describe your relationship with your boyfriend or girlfriend? If not, do you see these trends among any of your friends' relationships? Teen dating violence is real and dangerous. If you or someone you know is in an abusive relationship, please seek the help of a trusted adult.

Moving Too Fast

One minute you can be on your first date and the next minute you're being pressured to do something you're not ready for, like having sex. Abusive partners can coerce you into doing things you don't want to do. They may pour on the guilt by insinuating if you really love or care for them, you'll do what they want. Be careful to not buy into their deceptive lies.

Suffocating Paranoia

An abusive partner's paranoia can suck the breath right out of you. That person's emotional insecurity leads to distrust, which in turn can lead to constant surveillance. If you can't make a call, text or even hiccup without your boyfriend or girlfriend knowing, then you may have a stalker and not a partner.

Severing Relationships

People who abuse are often extremely jealous and insecure. In an effort to get you all to themselves, they will monopolize your time and push away friends and family. Unfortunately, you may not even realize what's happening until you're in over your head.

Domineering and Possessive

Power and control are at the heart of teen dating violence. Abusive partners are very possessive. They will go to great lengths and use any means necessary to keep you close and control you.

Throwing Verbal and Physical Jabs

Abusive partners prey upon your weaknesses. They use humiliation, put-downs and insults to dig at your feelings of self-worth. As a means to bolster their own confidence, they may use you as a verbal and physical punching bag. Don't stay in a relationship that tears you down rather than building you up.

For Parents: Watch for These Dating Abuse Signs

Parents, if your gut is telling you something isn't right with your teen's relationship, take heed. The following are some tell-tale signs of abuse:

Unexplainable Bumps and Bruises

If your teen is constantly making excuses for injuries, and the stories don't line up with the injury, be suspicious. Keep probing to see what your teen is covering up and who she or he may be trying to protect.

Depressed and Lonely

Is your teen becoming a hermit? Teens thrive on socialization and peer interaction. If your extraverted teen has suddenly become an introvert, that's reason for concern, since the effects of isolation on an adolescent can be detrimental.

Drug Use

Research finds having an abusive partner is associated a greater likelihood of substance use at the time of abuse. Not only are abusive partners using drugs, but so are victims. Oftentimes victims turn to substances as a means of coping and self-medication.

Declining Grades

A change in school performance can be a good indicator that something is wrong. According to the National Association of School Nurses, students who experienced physical or sexual violence had lower grades; approximately 20% had mostly D's or F's, while just six percent who had mostly A's. Dating violence has also been associated with truancy and dropping out of school.

Lack of Self-Care

Have you noticed your teen's hygiene, sleep and eating habits are drastically changing? Poor self-care is a sign that something significant is going on in your teen's life, even if they don't say anything about it.

Sneaky and Secretive

Is your teen spending an unhealthy amount of time with his girlfriend? Have you caught your teen in lies, such as regarding her whereabouts, calling in sick to work or skipping school? If so, be wary. If you feel your teen is keeping something from you, you're probably right; 67% of teens keep an abusive relationship secret.

Unhealthy relationships can start early and last a lifetime. Teens often think some behaviors, like teasing and name-calling, are a "normal" part of a relationship. However, these behaviors can become abusive and develop into more serious forms of violence.

Good Advice for Parents

Teens and tweens in relationships are most likely to discuss their experiences with friends and parents. But the older a child gets, the less likely she or he will talk to a parent.

- 67% of tweens in relationships discuss their experiences with friends.
- 67% of tweens in relationships discuss their experiences with their mom.
- 78% of teens discuss their dating relationships with friends.
- 48% of teens discuss their dating relationships with their mom.

Parents who delay talking to their tweens about relationships may find themselves out of the loop later on. Approximately 70% of parents who haven't talked to their tween say it's because their child is too young.

- ➢ 67% of parents say they know "a lot" or "everything" about their tween's dating relationship, but only 51% of tweens agree.

- ➢ 20% of tweens say their parents know little or nothing about their dating relationships, although only eight percent of parents admit that.

- ➢ 38% of parents say their tween has been in a relationship, whereas 47% of tweens say that about themselves.

- ➢ Only eight percent of parents say that their child has "hooked up" with a partner, versus seventeen percent of tweens who say they've "hooked up."

For parents, educators, and other adults concerned by these findings, two factors clearly have impact on the incidence of tween and teen dating abuse:

- ➢ Delaying the age at which a teenager first has sex greatly reduces the chances she or he will be involved in abuse.

- ➢ Talking to a child very early on about dating, relationships, and sexual behavior, even before it seems necessary, is essential to maintaining open communications between parent and child and may reduce the incidence of abuse.

Program Changes in the Definition of Rape

In December 2011, FBI Director Robert S. Mueller, III, approved revisions to the UCR Program's definition of rape: "Penetration, no matter how slight, of the vagina or anus with any body part or object, or oral penetration by a sex organ of another person, without the consent of the victim.

18 – Worst Possible Candidates

In this very short chapter we'll get straight to the point and list what to look for in the worst desirable candidates. The top ten in my book. In comparison, these candidates are much worse than a least desirable candidate (see the next Chapter 19: Least Desirable Candidates), and far removed from the best possible candidates (see Chapter 20: Best Possible Candidates).

The worst possible candidates and unworthy of dating your daughter and to be avoided at all costs. They're not for your daughter or you as a parent to fix. If you're not sure of their status running down the list, you might want to perform a background check to remove any doubt in your mind, and your daughter's too, that any potential candidate is without fail, a "Candidon't."

1. *A Sexual Harasser, Misogynist or Rapist*

2. *Has Violent Tendencies*

3. *A Gang Banger*

4. *A Juvenile Delinquent*

5. *A Bad Boy*

6. *A Highschool Drop Out*

7. ***Has an STD or STI***

8. ***He's Promiscuous***

9. ***Got Someone Pregnant***

10. ***He's a Sagger or a Tagger***

All of these worst possible candidate traits have been covered to one degree or another in other chapters. For the ones you're not sure of, I think the list above by itself covers them, and most of you should have a good idea of who and what they are. However, if your daughter is unsure of what they are, please inform and advise her on your own terms, and if you're unsure of some of them, brush up on what they are from the previous chapters.

19 – Least Desirable Candidates

Like the previous chapter, in this very short one we'll get straight to the point and list what to look for in the least desirable candidates. The top ten in my book. In comparison, these candidates may or may not, depending on the candidate, have the potential to elevate themselves to the best possible candidate status as outlined in Chapter 20: Best Possible Candidates.

For the most part, the least desirable candidates are also unworthy of dating your daughter, however, there might be some exceptions. Like the worst possible candidates, they're not your responsibility or your daughter to fix. However, under the right conditions, they could end up changing their status from a candidon't to a candidate.

1. *Wolf Hiding in Sheep's Clothing*

2. *High Risk Factor for Causing Teen Pregnancies*

3. *A Tobacco, Drug and Alcohol Abuser*

4. *Has Controlling Tendencies*

5. *Academic Under Performer*

6. *He Flunks the Three A's (Attitude, Appearance & Attire)*

7. **Has Family Risk Factors**

8. **Has Social Risk Factors**

9. **Hip Hop Gangsta' Wannabee**

10. **Questionable Social Media Type Postings**

All of these least desirable candidate traits have been covered to one degree or another in other chapters. For the ones you're not sure of, I think the list above by itself covers them, and most of you should have a good idea of who and what they are. However, if your daughter is unsure of what they are, please inform and advise her on your own terms, and if you're unsure of some of them, brush up on what they are from the previous chapters.

20 – Best Possible Candidates

Like the previous two chapters, this will also be very short one we'll get straight to the point and list what to look for in the best possible candidates. The top ten in my book. In comparison, these candidates are worthy of dating your daughter, provided they still pass the same rules and requirements for meeting the parents and accepting and acknowledging the do's and don'ts for dating your daughter.

These are the candidates your daughter should be looking for and/or accepting their offers to date, provide they meet her own personal requirements. These candidates have the potential for healthy and long-term relationships. They should provide safe and sane dating experiences for your daughter, and less involvement on the dad's and parent's part. So, let's see what traits separate these gentleman from the rest.

1. *Pursuit of Educational Excellence*

2. *A Gentleman and Always Faithful*

3. *He is Trustworthy*

4. *He is Respectful*

5. *He is Responsible*

6. *He Believes in Fairness*

7. *He is a Caring Person*

8. *He Practices Strong Citizenship*

9. *He Strives for Sapience*

10. *Being Religious is a Good Quality*

All of these best possible candidate traits have been covered in other chapters and should be apparent to everyone reading this book by now. In a world and society devoid of young men and adolescents of character, these are the role models for all the rest. Like everything worth perfecting, you have to work at it. If you don't, you might backslide and be relegated to the least desirable, and heaven forbid, the worst desirable category.

21 – The End of Innocence

There's a reason we end this journey at Chapter 21: The End of Innocence, because for most adolescents, the age of twenty-one is the last portal to adulthood.

Many adults are uncomfortable with the idea of teen sexuality and prefer to remain in ignorance or denial. But sexual activity is a part of human development, and tweens, teens, and young adults need access to comprehensive and non-stigmatizing information about sexual and reproductive health.

To one degree to another most parents are unable to control their teens. Regardless of your level of control, as noted before, the many benefits of open lines of communication can help them be more aware of the dangers of dating, relationships, and what their maturing bodies are capable of.

Making poor choices can have serious consequences that can affect their lives forever, and the lives of their parents as well. As noted throughout your journey through this book, it's essential to establish an open and honest dialogue in your home about sexual matters.

A Father's Rulebook on the Do's and Don'ts for Dating His Little Princess

Sound Advice for Dealing with Sexually Active Teens

Begin by asking your teenage girl to share her feelings about sex and having multiple partners. Show genuine interest by not arguing, lecturing, criticizing, attempting to control her or calling her derogatory names. Listen with empathy and understanding, even if you hold a different point of view.

Criticizing her could cause her to feel shame and guilt and lead her to refuse to talk to you in the future. Stress that you're aware that she's exploring her sexuality and you'll always love her unconditionally. Teenagers whose parents show unconditional love and support have fewer sexual partners than other teens, according to Planned Parenthood.

Share your own values about love, sex and intimacy. Tell her about some of your early sexual experiences and any valuable lessons you learned. Explain how sex is more meaningful in committed, loving relationships than with many different partners. Let her know what a healthy relationship consists of; such as respect, honesty, trust, equality and sexual intimacy; and those are the qualities you hope she finds in a partner.

By stressing the value of saving sex for healthy relationships, you can strengthen her resolve to avoid engaging in sex for less important reasons, such as peer pressure, according to Terri Apter, PhD, a University of Cambridge researcher and mother and teen expert. Devise strategies to help her resist sexual pressure. Go through different situations and practice how she should say "no" to sexual propositions.

Inform her about the dangers of promiscuous sex, such as sexually transmitted diseases (STDs) and pregnancy. Quote some sobering facts that pregnant teens are more likely to be high school dropouts, suffer economic hardship and be unhappy, according to Planned Parenthood. STDs can lead to life-threatening illnesses, such as AIDS and genital cancers.

Ask if she's using birth control. If not, make an immediate appointment for her to see a gynecologist and also get tested for STDs. Each year, there are approximately nineteen million cases of STDs reported, and half of them appear in young people who are 15 - 24 years old, according to the Centers for Disease Control and Prevention.

On Average: How Often Are Teens Having Sex?

Overall, teenagers had a median age at first sex of 16.9 years. Black males had the lowest observed median (15.0), and Asian American males the highest (18.1); white and Hispanic males, and white and black females, reported similar ages (about 16.5 years). Hispanic and Asian American females had rates of first sex about half that of white females, although these protective effects were explained by differences in family structure.

Even after controlling for other factors, black males had rates of first sex that were about 3-5 times the rates of the other gender-and-ethnicity groups. In addition, Asian American males were less likely than Hispanic males to be sexually experienced, and Hispanic males had almost twice the rates of sexual activity of Hispanic females.

In 2011–2013, among unmarried 15 - 19-year-olds, 44% of females and 49% of males had had sexual intercourse. These levels have remained steady since 2002. Adolescent sexual activity may include behaviors other than vaginal intercourse such as Abstinence and Outercourse as noted by Planned Parenthood.

In 2006–2010, the most common reason that sexually inexperienced adolescents aged 15 - 19 gave for not having had sex was that it was "against religion or morals" (41% of females and 31% of males). The second and third most common reasons were not having found the right person and wanting to avoid pregnancy.

Among sexually experienced adolescents aged 15 - 19, 73% of females and 58% of males reported in 2006–2010 that their first sexual experience was with a steady partner, cohabitor, fiancé or spouse. Sixteen percent of females and 28% of males reported having first had sex with someone they had just met or who was just a friend.

Adolescent sexual intercourse is increasingly likely to be described as wanted. First sex was described as wanted by 34% of women aged 18 - 24 in 2002 who had had sex before age twenty and by 41% in 2006–2010. Among men in the same age group, the share reporting first sex before age twenty as wanted increased from 43% to 62%.

Sex Education, Safe Sex and Contraceptive Use

The benefits of sex education, planned parenthood, and pregnancy and STI prevention were discussed in earlier chapters. This chapter will cover more about contraceptive use, accepting the fact that by the time your adolescent turns twenty-one, they will have had sex in at least one way or another.

A clear majority of studies and statistics show that most teenagers and young adults will not be abstinent or limit their sexual encounters to outercourse. Instead, they will have sex whether their parents want them to or not. So, there should be a back-up plan, multiple options, plenty of sex education, open communication, and easy access to contraceptives to effectively deal with the inevitable and end of innocence.

Other Options for Intimacy Without Having Sex

Sexual intercourse is not the only way two people can get to know each other and being intimate. Too often, people opt for intimacy through sex, only to regret the decision later, because they did so, not really know each other first. Intimacy can be developed through a variety of means and methods such as:

- ➢ Talking and listening.

- ➢ Sharing joys, hurts, dreams, goals, wishes and other aspects of life.

- Honesty and respect for one another.
- Having fun and playing together.

Abstinence is chosen by women and men for a number of reasons. If you are a teenager, it is the best way to avoid being a pregnant teen or getting a STD. Some of the reasons people choose abstinence are for a variety of reasons as noted below:

- Honor of personal, moral, or religious beliefs.
- Wait until they are married and in a monogamous and committed relationship.
- Pursue school, career, and other activities.

To avoid pregnancy and sexually transmitted diseases, intimacy and affection can be expressed in many ways other than sexual intercourse. Kissing, hugging, massaging, and holding hands are some of the ways that couples express their affection in a physical manner.

The caution with any physical affection is that it can lead to passion and a desire for something more. Intimacy and affection can also be expressed in other ways such as:

- Conversations.
- Cards, letters, and love notes.
- Support in your partner's activities.
- Creative and fun dating.

What is Abstinence?

The definition of abstinence is when you don't have sex. Outercourse is other sexual activities besides vaginal sex. Sexual abstinence and outercourse (see below) can mean different things to different people. People are abstinent for lots of different reasons.

Sometimes people use abstinence as birth control to prevent pregnancy.

Abstinence can mean different things depending on who you ask. Many people say abstinence is not doing any kind of sexual activity with another person, including vaginal, oral, and anal sex. That's what we're calling abstinence here.

Abstinence prevents pregnancy by keeping semen away from the vagina, so the sperm cells in semen can't get to an egg and cause pregnancy. If you're abstinent 100% of the time, pregnancy can't happen. Period!

People sometimes only use abstinence to prevent pregnancy on days they're fertile (most likely to get pregnant), but they may have vaginal sex at other times. This is called fertility-awareness.

Anybody can be abstinent, no matter your age, gender, sexuality, or the sexual experiences you've had before. People are abstinent off and on for reasons that may change over time, and a few are abstinent their whole lives. You can choose to be abstinent whenever you want, even if you've had sex before. Some could end up as the 40-year old virgin!

Meaningful Relationships and the Abstinence POV

Abstinence simply means not having sex and refraining from sexual intercourse. For most people, abstinence is the absence of sexual contact altogether. It is the healthiest way to avoid a teen pregnancy and more importantly, the best way to avoid contracting an STI. Abstinence prevents pregnancy 100% of the time when practiced consistently. It is the most effective form of birth control.

Abstinence prevents pregnancy because sexual intercourse does not take place. It involves refraining from any activity that leads to an exchange of body fluids. Periodic abstinence is often used by couples who are practicing the fertility awareness method of birth control as a means of preventing pregnancy during the fertile period of a woman's cycle.

There are no side effects or health risks related to abstinence. Abstinence prevents the transmission of sexually transmitted infections 100% of the time when practiced appropriately and consistently. Abstinence is most successful when you are diligent and use planning within your relationships. To make it easier, try some of the following ideas:

- ➢ Do things with friends or in groups.
- ➢ Go on double dates.
- ➢ Minimize physical affection that could lead to passion and desire, making it harder to abstain from sexual intercourse.
- ➢ Avoid situations where you are alone.

Relationships that involve sexual intercourse are filled with physical, emotional, and psychological risks. Abstinence provides teenagers the opportunity to avoid those risks. Individuals who abstain from sexual intercourse during their teenage years tend to have fewer sexual partners in the future.

Remaining abstinent as a teenager means that you will be less likely to contract a sexually transmitted disease, which may also lead to infertility, develop cancer of the cervix and experience an unplanned pregnancy.

How Does Outercourse Work?

Many couples want to be sexual with each other without having vaginal sex and/or risking pregnancy. Outercourse can prevent pregnancy the same way abstinence does by keeping sperm away from an egg.

Using outercourse as birth control means you do some sexual activities, but you don't have vaginal sex (penis-in-vagina) or get any semen (cum) in the vagina. This way, the sperm cells in semen can't get to an egg and cause pregnancy. Some outercourse examples include kissing, massage, masturbating, dry humping (grinding), and talking about your fantasies.

People may also choose to have oral sex and/or anal sex. Oral sex won't lead to pregnancy, and anal sex doesn't cause pregnancy either (unless semen spills out into the vagina). But both anal and oral sex can spread STDs, so use a condom during oral sex and anal sex if that's your goal or preference.

What Are the Pros and Cons of Abstinence and Outercourse?

The pros of abstinence and outercourse include:

- Has no side effects or health risks.
- Prevents pregnancy and the transmission of sexually transmitted diseases.
- It's free!
- Reduces emotional and psychological challenges related to relationships that involve sexual activity.

The cons of abstinence and outercourse include:

- Requires willpower and discipline.
- Both partners must be equally committed.

But in the United States, 46% of all high school age students, and 62% of high school seniors, have had sexual intercourse; almost nine million teens have already had sex. It is critically important for adults to address adolescent sexuality realistically and to recognize that many factors, including socioeconomic status, race or ethnicity, family structure, educational aspirations, and life experiences, affect young people's behavior and choices.

At the heart of waiting until marriage is a yearning for greater meaning in all things, most of all marriage. The end-goal of waiting is achieving a more meaningful marriage, but this ambition will trickle down into the friendship and dating relationships you enter into before marriage as well. People who wait till marriage tend to prioritize meaningfulness in all relationships much more than other people.

One-night stands, casual flings, superficial friendships, these will be entirely foreign (and appalling) concepts to you if this is your goal or preference. You pursue closeness and meaning in every relationship you have, platonic or otherwise. Now, this doesn't mean that you will get deep meaning out of every relationship, just that you will try to get it. You'll rarely be comfortable with a friendship or a dating relationship in which you don't get to know the person very well.

For the ones that you do know well, you will get the maximum potential out of every relationship. Sometimes that won't amount to much. Sometimes it will amount to everything. And that's the good news when you aim for depth and meaning, you will frequently get it. Or, you'll move on until you do.

Pregnancy

In 2013, the adolescent pregnancy rate reached a record low of 43 pregnancies per 1,000 women aged 15 - 19, indicating that less than five percent of females in this age-group became pregnant. This rate represented a decline to just over one-third of the peak rate of 118 per 1,000, which occurred in 1990.

In 2013, about 448,000 U.S. women aged 15 - 19 became pregnant. Seventy-two percent of adolescent pregnancies occurred among the oldest age-group (18 - 19-year-olds). Pregnancies are much less common among females younger than fifteen. In 2013, four pregnancies occurred per 1,000 females aged fourteen or younger. In other words, about 0.4% of adolescents younger than fifteen became pregnant that year.

In 2013, black and Hispanic adolescents had pregnancy rates of 75 and 61 per 1,000 women aged 15 - 19, respectively; white adolescents had a pregnancy rate of 30 per 1,000. As noted many times, despite recent declines, the U.S. adolescent pregnancy rate continues to be one of the highest among developed countries for this reason and others.

Nationally, seventy-five percent of pregnancies among 15 - 19-year-olds were unintended (meaning either mistimed or unwanted) in 2008–2011, and adolescents account for about fifteen percent of all unintended pregnancies annually. Sixty-one percent of pregnancies among 15 - 19-year-olds in 2013 ended in births, while 24% ended in abortions and the rest in miscarriages.

Abortion

Although federal funds are not permitted to cover abortion services in most cases, some states and private insurance plans do allow insurance coverage of abortions. However, some minors with coverage may not use insurance to access abortion services because they are not aware that these services are covered or because of confidentiality concerns.

Women aged 15 - 19 had just under 110,000 abortions in 2013. About eleven percent of all abortions that year were obtained by adolescents. In 2013, there were eleven abortions for every 1,000 women aged 15 - 19. This is the lowest rate observed since abortion was legalized nationwide in 1973, and just one-fourth of the peak rate in 1988.

Between 1985 and 2007, the proportion of pregnancies among 15 - 19-year-old women (excluding miscarriages) that ended in abortion declined by one-third, from 46% to 31%. This proportion has remained relatively stable since 2007.

The reasons women younger than twenty most frequently give for having an abortion are concerns about how having a baby would negatively change their lives, inability to afford a baby now and not feeling mature enough to raise a child.

As of July 2017, laws in 37 states required that a minor seeking an abortion involve one or both parents in the decision.

Childbearing

In 2013, women aged nineteen or younger had 276,000 births, representing seven percent of all U.S. births. By the age of twenty, one in three women will have become pregnant and most will be unmarried. This is a shocking statistic that needs to change!

In 2013, there were 26 births per 1,000 women aged 15 - 19; this rate marked a more than 50% decline from the peak rate of 62 births per 1,000, reached in 1991. Evidence suggests that this decline is primarily attributable to increases in adolescents' contraceptive use; declines in sexual activity played a smaller role.

Most births to adolescent mothers are first births. In 2013, seventeen percent of births to women aged 15 - 19 were second or higher-order births.

Nearly all births among women aged 15 - 19 occur outside of marriage, 89% in 2013, up from 79% in 2000. Yet, over the last several decades, adolescents' share of nonmarital births among all age-groups has declined, from 52% in 1975 to fifteen percent in 2013.

Between 1991 and 2014, childbearing among young men declined 54%, from 25 births per 1,000 males aged 15 – 19 to eleven births per 1,000. Among men in this age-group in 2014, 27% reported that the pregnancy was intended.

The rates of childbearing among young men vary considerably by race. In 2014, the rate among black males aged 15 - 19 (19 per 1,000) was almost twice that among their white counterparts (10 per 1,000).

Well, that's the end. I hope it was a worthwhile read and that your daughter has a safe and sane journey through her dating years, and the two of you get through it just fine. Best regards and good luck!

Closing

You heard me say that my mom was a Playboy Bunny? Well it's true, and as the "oldest man in the house" of a single mother (I was a precocious boy of ten), it was my job to help zip-up her bunny outfit in the back when her zipper got stuck. Single and free to do most anything she wanted to and to date anyone she wanted to, my mom did just that, dating dozens of playboys from the Playboy Club.

Hoping one day she would fall in love with one of them, and he with her, and get married, and I would have a dad again, it never came to be. However, what did come to be was that I developed an advanced sexual knowledge at an early age, observed many playboy tactics and dating techniques tried on my mother, and eventually became a playboy of sorts myself when I grew into manhood.

If you're thinking what I'm thinking, 'I'm the wrong person to be writing a book like this, right?' Well maybe not! Just think about it for a minute. Have you ever heard or read stories about the ex-hacker now doing cyber intelligence for the CIA, or the high-profile thief who now designs surveillance/security systems, or the diehard gangster who is now reformed and dedicated his life to preaching the word of the gospel?

With a PhD in life (my PhD stands for personal human drama) who better to know every young man's or boy's playbook for scoring on a daughter? Whether it's your daughter, another teenage daughter, or an anonymous young woman; I've played both offense and now defense, so to speak, on the dating game playing field, and I know every play in the playbook, from the big league to the little league. So, who better than me to protect your daughter and ensure she's experiencing safe and sane dating?

I'd take a bullet for my daughter, and most dads would too. With that said, if you don't like some of my "tough love" advice and straight-forward statistics because they demonstrate and acknowledge there are many noticeable and, in some cases, significant differences in certain racial, religious, and ethnic groups when it comes to teenager behavior and dating practices, too bad!

If these inconvenient truths are hard to accept or follow and you continue to point the finger of accusation and express such non-sensical things like, "he's old school!" or "he's prejudice!" or "he's a racist!" etc., etc., etc., you need to read on to the next page, then to the Afterword and over to my Biography for the facts and history that prove otherwise.

When you've circled back to this page, hopefully, you'll come to the realization that you've been hypocritical and the problem most likely lies with you. If you want to be part of the solution, and not the problem, you need to identify and accept the problem, and then start working on the solutions to fix them.

Trying to shoot the messenger, does you and society no benefit, in fact it does more harm. If you truly want to benefit society and are capable of rational thought, as a sapient being, and desire to be part of the solution, there's a place for you at the non-profit organization SAPIENT Being at their website at www.SAPIENTBeing.org.

Check it out and see if you're ready and wise enough to join the **S**ociety **A**dvancing **P**ersonal **I**ntelligence and **E**nlightenment **N**ow **T**ogether, the **S.A.P.I.E.N.T. Being** and elevate yourself to a higher state of being.

A Father's Rulebook on the Do's and Don'ts for Dating His Little Princess

Afterword

Unfortunately, we live in a world these day gone mad and turned upside down it seems. It's much easier these days to shoot the messenger and suppress free speech by labeling them all sorts of things that they're not. Much like a witch-hunt, or where you're guilty first until proven innocent later, or simply a lack of free speech, many people cannot seem to separate their opinions from facts. It's madness!

As the time-tested saying goes, "Everyone is entitled to their own opinions, but they're not entitled to their own facts." Facts are facts, but they can be skewed and manipulated for disingenuous methods and false narratives. We don't do that at Fratire Publishing! In fact, we'll go out of our way to point out and correct such fallacies. This is part of the higher calling of being a sapient being.

So be careful out there with the accusations and finger pointing, because I have a favorite saying and demonstration that stops them cold in their tracks. And here it is: When you point that finger of accusation(s), it's been my long and traveled experience in life and sapience, to notice that the people doing the finger pointing have their other four fingers pointing right back at them. It wasn't always so!

It's also been my experience in life that these kinds of ludicrous and nonsensical comments say more about the prejudice, cluelessness, naivety, immaturity, hypocrisy, hatred, bias, etc. etc. etc. of the accuser than the accused. It seems like so many of us have tossed aside all reason, logic and common sense, and given in to their illogical and irrational emotions where fiction is fact and facts are denied and worst of all; no free speech allowed.

Sincerely,

Corey Lee Wilson
Publisher & Author

A Father's Rulebook on the Do's and Don'ts for Dating His Little Princess

Appendix

Father/Daughter & Mother/Son Dance
https://www.youtube.com/watch?v=jFXAI_EEbQE

"So You Want to Date My Daughter? A Father's Rulebook on the Do's and Don'ts for Dating His Little Princess" video at:
http://youtu.be/ZqBSL40PhIwn

"Watch This Woman Receive 100 Catcalls While Walking Around for a Day" video at:
http://www.huffingtonpost.com/2014/10/28/walking-in-nyc-as-a-woman_n_6063054.html?utm_hp_ref=mostpopular

Application Form for Permission to Date My Daughter:
For an electronic copy in Word or pdf format, please visit my website at www.SYWTDMD.net and go to the Contact page and fill out that info form so you can receive the Application Form for Permission to Date My Daughter form.

Permission to Date My Daughter Contract and Agreement Form: For an electronic copy in Word or pdf format, please visit my website at www.SYWTDMD.net and go to the Contact page and fill out that info form so you can receive the Application Form for Permission to Date My Daughter form.

Glossary – Dating Slang and Teenage Jargon

If you hear a lot of these words below coming from your daughter's date or read them in his application form, you might want to pay closer attention to what he is saying or stating and be aware that he might not be the right date for your daughter. If all of his slang and jargon begins to sound like gangsta' talk (see definition below), you can be 100% sure he is not the right candidate for your daughter and never will be.

Bootylicious – Used to describe how very fine someone looks, particularly their ass.

Crib – A boy's room, pad, apartment, or make out place.

Diva – A girl who thinks she's a rock star.

Double date – When two or more couples go out on a date together.

Dudette – The feminine name for dude. One who is hip or cool.

Dumped – To get turned down on a date.

Freak Dancing – Also known as grinding or freaking or wining (in the Caribbean), is a type of close partner dance where two or more dancers rub their bodies against each other.

Gangsta' – A real thug, livin' the streets the way that the hip-hop lifestyle would suggest.

A Father's Rulebook on the Do's and Don'ts for Dating His Little Princess

Grinding - Also known as freak dancing or freaking or wining (in the Caribbean), is a type of close partner dance where two or more dancers rub their bodies against each other.

Himbo – Male bimbo.

Ho' – Street term for a whore.

Homie – Gangster or rap term for a fellow member or a friend.

Hooking up – Means as little as just getting together or as much as having sex together.

Mackin' out – Making out with.

Making out – Kissing and fondling.

Mallrat – A person who spends much of their free time at the mall, not necessarily buying anything or working.

Negging – The offering of low-grade insults meant to undermine the self-confidence of a woman, so she might be more vulnerable to your advances.

Player – A boy who is sexually active and desirous of and/or dating many girls at the same time.

Posse – A fraternity, group, or gang of like-minded boys who hang out together.

Rave – An all-night party.

Reputation – Something easily lost when going out with the wrong boy.

Sagging or **Saggin'**- Is a manner of wearing trousers (slacks, shorts, pants or jeans) below the waist, revealing much of the underwear.

Sexting – E-mailing nude pictures of yourself to others.

Slore – A slut and a whore combined.

Slut – A girl who gets around and has sex with many different boys.

STDs – Sexually transmitted diseases.

STIs – Sexually transmitted infections.

TDV – Teen dating violence.

Tease – A girl who leads a boy on.

Teenager – An adolescent or teen typically between the ages of 13 - 18.

Tween – An adolescent typically between the ages of 10 - 12.

A Father's Rulebook on the Do's and Don'ts for Dating His Little Princess

Resources

"10 Old-Fashioned Dating Habits We Should Bring Back." 31 May 2014. *BeLikeWaterProduction.com.* http://belikewaterproduction.com/2014/05/31/10-old-fashioned-dating-habits-we-should-bring-back/

"Adolescent Development and STDs." U.S. Dept. of Health & Human Services. 12 Sep. 2016. *HHS.gov.* https://www.hhs.gov/ash/oah/adolescent-development/reproductive-health-and-teen-pregnancy/stds/index.html

"Adolescent Sexual and Reproductive Health in the United States." Sep. 2016. *Guttmacher.org.* https://www.guttmacher.org/fact-sheet/american-teens-sexual-and-reproductive-health?gclid=CjwKCAiAmvjR-BRBlEiwAWFc1mPPTsj4V6V0qE7rBHIaI4srYzm4zOzLn-lYXOht2QOjTWyiVPr80GgBoCPWwQAvD_BwE

"Adolescent Sexual Behavior: Demographics." Feb. 2012. *AdvocatesforYouths.org.* http://www.advocatesforyouth.org/publications/publications-a-z/413-adolescent-sexual-behavior-i-demographics

"Are We Closing the School Discipline Gap?" Feb. 2015. The Center for Civil Rights Remedies. https://civilrightsproject.ucla.edu/resources/projects/center-for-civil-rights-remedies/school-to-prison-folder/federal-reports/are-we-closing-the-school-discipline-gap/AreWeClosingTheSchoolDisciplineGap_FINAL221.pdf

Bailey, Kate. "10 Old Fashioned Dating Habits We Should Make Cool Again." 4 Dec. 2013. *ThoughtCatalog.com.*

http://thoughtcatalog.com/kate-bailey/2013/12/10-old-fashioned-dating-habits-we-should-make-cool-again/

Bates, Daniel. "Children Who Start Dating Too Young Are More Likely to Have Behavioral Problems Than Those Who Wait for Love." 1 Oct. 2013. *DailyMail.com*. http://www.dailymail.co.uk/news/article-2440182/Children-start-dating-young-likely-behavioural-problems-wait-love-says-study.html

Bennett, Jonathan. "Bad Boy Syndrome." 25 Jul. 2017. *The PopularMan.com*.

Blau, Liz. "How to Help Promiscuous Teen Girls." 13 Jun. 2017. *LiveStrong.com*. https://www.livestrong.com/article/560028-how-to-help-promiscuous-teen-girls/

Borba Ed.D., Michele. *The Big Book of Parenting Solutions: 101 Answers to Your Everyday Challenges and Wildest Worries* San Francisco: Jossey-Bass, 2009.

Brian, Marshall. *The Teenager's Guide to the Real World: How to Become a Successful Adult* Raleigh: BYG Publishing, Inc., 1997.

Budd, Joel & Linda, *So You Want to Date My Daughter? A Program for Dating with Destiny in Mind* Tulsa: Cross Staff Publishing, 2008.

Cameron, W. Bruce. *8 Simple Rules for Dating My Teenage Daughter: And Other Tips from a Beleaguered Father* New York: Workman Publishing, 2001.

Character Counts, Six Pillars of Character. https://character-counts.org/program-overview/six-pillars/

"Child Development: Teenagers (15-17 Years of Age)." Dec. 2017. *Centers for Disease Control & Prevention (CDC)*.

"Child Development: Young Teens (12-14 Years of Age)." Dec. 2017. *Centers for Disease Control & Prevention (CDC)*. https://www.cdc.gov/ncbddd/childdevelopment/positiveparenting/adolescence.html

"Church Attendance Boosts Student GPAs." 22 Aug. 2008. Live Science. *FoxNews.com*. http://www.foxnews.com/story/0,2933,409121,00.html

Cladwell Team. "How To: Pull Your Pants Up (A Brief History of Saggy Pants)." Jan. 2018. https://cladwell.com/blog/pull-your-pants-up-a-brief-history-of-saggy-pants/

Conklin, MPH, MCHES, Kurt. "American Adolescents' Sources of Sexual Health Information." Dec. 2017. *Guttmacher.org*. https://www.guttmacher.org/sites/default/files/factsheet/facts-american-teens-sources-information-about-sex.pdf

"Date Ideas – Creative Date Ideas for Every Occasion." http://niftydateideas.blogspot.com/ (Jan. 2015)

"Dating 101: The Basics of Dating." *Date.Lifetips.com*.

"Dating Abuse Statistics." LoveIsRespect.org. http://www.loveisrespect.org/ (Jan. 2018)

"Dear Dish-It: Am I Too Young to Date?" *KidzWorld.com*. http://www.kidzworld.com/article/19580-dear-dish-it-am-i-too-young-to-date (Jan. 2015)

"Delinquent Behavior Among Boys 'Contagious,' Study Finds." 17 Jul. 2009. *ScienceDaily.com*. https://www.sciencedaily.com/releases/2009/07/090716113301.htm

Demby, Gene. "Sagging Pants and the Long History Of 'Dangerous' Street Fashion." 11 Sep. 2014. *NPR.org*. https://www.npr.org/sections/codeswitch/2014/09/11/347143588/sagging-pants-and-the-long-history-of-dangerous-street-fashion

"Different Types of Parenting Styles and Their Effects on Teens." 9 Oct. 2017. *SecureTeen.com*. https://www.secureteen.com/parenting-style/different-types-of-parenting-styles-and-their-effects-on-teens/

Dr. Phil. "How to Talk to Your Daughter About Sex" *DrPhil.com*. http://www.drphil.com/articles/article/162 (Jan. 2015)

"Emotional Pressures of Single Parenting on Teens." 12 Aug. 2013. *SecureTeen.com*. https://www.secureteen.com/single-dad/emotional-pressures-of-single-parenting-on-teens/

Fabius, Carine. "The Attraction to Bad Boys Explained." 13 Nov. 2012. *HuffingtonPost.com.* https://www.huffingtonpost.com/carine-fabius/bad-boy-syndrome_b_2110970.html

Fagan, Dr. Center for Research on Marriage and Religion; Marriage and Religion Research Institute in Washington, D.C. 15 Apr. 2003. *LifeSiteNews.com*

Ferrara, Dr. F. Felicia. "How to Encourage Responsible Teen Dating." *eHow.com.* http://www.ehow.com/video_4971164_encourage-responsible-teen-dating.html (Mar. 2012)

Fox, Annie M.Ed. *The Teen Survival Guide to Dating & Relating* Minneapolis: Free Spirit Publishing Inc., 2005.

Glauber, Anne. "Tween and Teen Dating Violence and Abuse Study." Feb. 2008. The National Domestic Violence Hotline. https://www.haven-oakland.org/assets/media/pdf/tru-tween-teen-study-feb-081.pdf

Grover, Sam. "Tips on First Dates for Shy Girls." 23 May 2011. *OurEverydayLife.com.* http://www.ehow.com/info_8477127_tips-first-dates-shy-girls.html

Gunz (reposted by Gawfer). "Wanna Date My Daughter, Heh?" 1 Sep. 2006. http://ebyzandgunz.blogspot.com/2006/09/wanna-date-my-daughter-heh.html and http://gawfer2001.blogspot.com/2006/09/so-you-want-to-date-my-daughter-eh.html

Ham, Becky. "Family History Influences Sexual Behavior in Black, Hispanic Teens." 2 Jan. 2003. Health Behavior News Service. *HBNS.org.* https://www.eurekalert.org/pub_releases/2003-01/cfta-fhi010203.php

"Health Disparities in HIV/AIDS, Viral Hepatitis, STDs, and TB: African American/Blacks." *Centers for Disease Control & Prevention (CDC).* http://www.cdc.gov/nchhstp/healthdisparities/AfricanAmericans.html (Jan. 2018)

"Health Disparities in HIV/AIDS, Viral Hepatitis, STDs, and TB: Hispanics/Latinos." *Centers for Disease Control & Prevention (CDC).* http://www.cdc.gov/nchhstp/healthdisparities/Hispanics.html (Jan. 2018)

A Father's Rulebook on the Do's and Don'ts for Dating His Little Princess

"Help for Single Mom's Raising Defiant Teens." *OnlineParentingCoach.com.* http://www.onlineparentingcoach.com/2013/07/help-for-single-moms-raising-defiant.html (Dec. 2017)

"How to Prevent Teens from Sexting." 21 May 2012. *MiddleEarthNJ.WordPress.com.* https://middleearthnj.wordpress.com/2012/05/21/how-to-prevent-teens-from-sexting/

'How to Talk to Your Kids About Sex." *ValuesParenting.com.*

http://date.lifetips.com/cat/989/teen-dating/index.html (Jan. 2015)

http://parents.berkeley.edu/advice/teens/parties.html

http://thepopularman.com/bad-boy-syndrome/

http://www.valuesparenting.com/talktokids.php (24 Mar. 2012)

https://lifestyle.howstuffworks.com/family/parenting/tweens-teens/teenager-is-promiscuous.htm (26 Oct. 2014)

https://www.cdc.gov/ncbddd/childdevelopment/positiveparenting/adolescence2.html

https://www.mocadsv.org/What-is-Teen-Dating-Violence-TDV/ (Jan. 2018)

https://www.thoughtco.com/facts-about-teen-dating-violence-abuse-3533771

"Is 12 Too Young to Start Dating?" 26 May 2010. *CBSNews.com.* http://www.cbsnews.com/news/is-12-too-young-to-start-dating/

Jander, Lisa. *Dater's Ed: The Instruction Manual for Parents* Lake Orion: Manna Enterprises, 2008.

Joseph, Jim. "Why Reputation Management Is Critical to Your Personal Brand." Contributor, Marketing Master - Author - Blogger – Dad. 9 Dec. 2013. https://www.entrepreneur.com/article/230187

Kerby, Rob. "Church Kids Less Likely to Divorce or Live in Poverty." 27 Aug. 2011.

http://blog.beliefnet.com/on_the_front_lines_of_the_culture_wars/2011/08/church-kids-are-less-likely-to-divorce-or-live-in-poverty.html

Kirberger, Kimberly. *Teen Lover Series on Relationships: A Book for Teenagers* Deerfield Beach: Health Communications, Inc., 1999.

Knudson, Michelle. "A Guide on How to Talk to Your Daughter About Dating." 17 Jul. 2006. *AssociatedContent.com.* http://voices.yahoo.com/a-guide-talk-daughter-dating-53338.html?cat=25

Lohmann, Raychelle Cassandra. "Teen Dating Violence: What Parents and Teens Should Know." 21 Feb. 2017. *USNews.com.* https://health.usnews.com/wellness/for-parents/articles/2017-02-21/teen-dating-violence-what-parents-and-teens-should-know

Lowen, Linda. "10 Facts About Teen Dating Violence - Teen Dating Abuse Statistics." 6 Nov. 2017. *ThoughtCo.com.* http://womensissues.about.com/od/datingandsex/a/TeenDatingAbuse.htm

Maffei, Michelle. "Should You Chaperone Your Teen's Prom? 6 Apr. 2011. *SheKnows.com.* http://www.sheknows.com/parenting/articles/827563/should-you-chaperone-your-teens-prom

Mancini, Lisa. "Father Absence and Its Effects on Daughters." Dissertation, Western Connecticut State University, 2010.

Marshall, Kristin. "7 Useful Tips for Meeting the Parents." 16 Mar. 2011. *OnLineDating.org.*

Masland, Molly. "Carnal Knowledge: The Sex Ed Debate." *MSNBC.com.* http://www.nbcnews.com/id/3071001/ns/health-childrens_health/t/carnal-knowledge-sex-ed-debate/ (Dec. 2017)

Matte, Christy. "Digital Parenting 101 - From Screen Time to Social Media." 17 Feb. 2017. *TheSpruce.com.* https://www.thespruce.com/digital-parenting-101-4038621

McCarthy, M.D., Claire. "Online Dating for Teens? Why Parents Need to Talk About Online Relationships." 30 Sep. 2013. *HuffingtonPost.com.* http://www.huffingtonpost.com/claire-mccarthy-md/online-dating-for-teens_b_3682486.html

Miller, Shane. "Sagging Pants, Negative Messages." May 2012. *BronxJournal.com.* http://bronxjournal.com/2012/05/sagging-pants-negative-messages/

Morin, Amy. "Tips for Establishing Dating Rules for Your Teen." 28 Mar. 2017. *VeryWell.com.* https://www.verywell.com/tips-for-establishing-dating-rules-for-your-teen-2611306

Morin, Amy. "When is Your Teen Ready for a Relationship." *VeryWell.com.* http://parentingteens.about.com/od/teensexuality/fl/When-is-Your-Teen-Ready-for-a-Relationship.htm (Jan. 2015)

Morvay, Reka. "About Teenage Online Dating." *eHow.com.* http://www.ehow.com/video_4754207_teenage-online-dating.html?ref=Track2&utm_source=ask (Mar. 2012)

"Negative Psychological Effects of a Single Parent Family on Children." 30 Aug. 2016. *SecureTeen.com.* https://www.secureteen.com/single-dad/negative-psychological-effects-of-a-single-parent-family-on-children/

"New CA Law: Teens Must Wait One Year Before Transporting Young Passengers." 28 Dec. 2005. *MotorTrend.com.* http://www.motortrend.com/auto_news/112_news051228_teendrivinglaw/viewall.html

Partridge, Dale. "4 Signs of a True Gentleman." 12 Oct. 2014. http://dalepartridge.com/4-signs-true-gentleman/

Payleitner, Jay. "Daddy-Daughter Date Ideas for Committed Dads." National Center for Fathering. *Fathers.com.* http://www.fathers.com/s7-hot-topics/c37-daughters/daddy-daughter-date-ideas-for-committed-dads-guest-blog/ (Feb. 2015)

Philby, Charlotte. "Teenage Dating Apps are Hunting Ground for Adult Abusers." 11 Aug. 2014. *Independent.co.uk.* http://www.independent.co.uk/life-style/gadgets-and-tech/news/teenage-dating-apps-are-hunting-ground-for-adult-abusers-9662817.html

Reeves, Richard V. and Halikias. "Race Gaps in SAT Scores Highlight Inequality and Hinder Upward Mobility." 1 Feb. 2017. *Brookings.edu.* https://www.brookings.edu/research/race-gaps-in-sat-scores-highlight-inequality-and-hinder-upward-mobility/

"Reporting Rape in 2013: Uniform Crime Reporting Program Changes Definition of Rape." 9 Apr. 2014. DOJ-FBI, Criminal Justice Information Services (CJIS) Division Uniform Crime Reporting (UCR) Program. https://ucr.fbi.gov/recent-program-updates/reporting-rape-in-2013

Rubin, Julia Lynn. "Kids Dating Too Young: Adolescents Who Date Early Twice as Likely to Develop Behavioral Problems." 1 Oct. 2013. *HNGN.com.* http://www.hngn.com/articles/13793/20131001/kids-dating-young-adolescents-who-date-early-twice-develop-behavioral.htm

Rudlin LCSW, Kathryn. "Risk Factors for Teen Pregnancy." 26 Jul. 2017. *VeryWell.com.* https://www.verywell.com/teen-pregnancy-risk-factors-2611269?print

Saltz, Dr. Gail. "Five Tips for Teen Dating." 24 Sep. 2003. *Today.com.* http://www.today.com/id/3088174/ns/today-parenting_and_family/t/five-tips-teen-dating/

Sayeed, Riaz. "A Father-Daughter Tipsheet on Dealing with the Prom." *SoundVision.com.* https://www.soundvision.com/article/a-father-daughter-tipsheet-on-dealing-with-the-prom (Mar. 2012)

"School Dances." Sep. 2008. Berkeley Parents Network. *CalParents.Berkeley.edu.* http://parents.berkeley.edu/advice/teens/schooldances.html

"Sexual and Reproductive Health of Persons Aged 10 - 24 Years - United States, 2002—2007." 17 Jul. 2009. *Centers for Disease Control & Prevention (CDC).* https://www.cdc.gov/mmwr/preview/mmwrhtml/ss5806a1.htm

"Sexually Active Teens." *TeenPregnancyStatistics.org.* http://www.teenpregnancystatistics.org/content/sexually-active-teens.html (Apr. 2011)

"Sexually Transmitted Diseases (STDs): CDC Fact Sheets." *Centers for Disease Control & Prevention (CDC).* https://www.cdc.gov/std/healthcomm/fact_sheets.htm (Jan. 2018)

"Sexually Transmitted Infection." 26 Dec. 2017. *Wikipedia.org.* https://en.wikipedia.org/wiki/Sexually_transmitted_infection

Siebold, Steve. "It's Time to Make Sex Education Mandatory in Our Nation's Schools." 9 Apr. 2013. *HuffingtonPost.com.* http://www.huffingtonpost.com/steve-siebold/sex-education-schools_b_3006483.html

A Father's Rulebook on the Do's and Don'ts for Dating His Little Princess

Sieczkowski, Cavan. "Watch This Woman Receive 100 Catcalls While Walking Around for A Day." 28 Oct. 2014. *Huffington Post.com*. http://www.huffingtonpost.com/2014/10/28/walking-in-nyc-as-a-woman_n_6063054.html?utm_hp_ref=mostpopular

"Single Parenting: Safeguard Your Teen's Future Relationships." 11 Nov. 2013. *SecureTeen.com*. https://www.secureteen.com/single-dad/single-parenting-safeguard-your-teen's-future-relationships/

"Stages of Adolescent Development" (Chart). 2008. Adapted from the American Academy of Child and Adolescent's Facts for Families.

Stambler, Deborah. "Date, Dress …Condom? Talking to Teens About Safety at Prom." 2 Apr. 2014. *Mom.me* http://mom.me/teen/11768-date-dresscondom-talking-teens-about-being-safe-prom/

Stannard, Dawn. "How to Cope When Your Teenager Starts Dating." 30 Oct. 2007. *DadCanDo.com*. http://www.dadcando.com/default_ARTICLE.asp?menuID=Boyfriend&catagory=Homepage&eaf=True (Dec. 2017)

"Teachers: Comprehensive Sex Ed." 18 Dec. 2017. *American Sexual Health Association (ASHA)*. SHASexualHealth.org/teachers/

"Teen Dating Sites & Social Networks." *AllOnlineDatingSited.com*. http://www.allonlinedatingsites.com/teen-dating-sites (10 Oct. 2014)

"Teen Dating Violence." Arkansas Coalition Against Domestic Violence (ACADV). https://www.domesticpeace.com/teen-dating-violence (Jan. 2018)

"Teen Dating Violence." City of Troy, Ohio. Jan. 2018. https://www.troyohio.gov/200/Teen-Dating-Violence

"The National Intimate Partner and Sexual Violence Survey (NISVS): 2010-2012 State Report." Apr. 2017. National Center for Injury Prevention and Control of the Centers for Disease Control and Prevention. https://www.cdc.gov/violenceprevention/pdf/NISVS-StateReportBook.pdf

"Teen Pregnancy Facts." *TeenPregnancyStatistics.org*. http://www.teenhelp.com/teen-pregnancy/teen-pregnancy-facts.html (Apr. 2011)

"Teen Pregnancy Risks." *TeenHelp.com*. http://www.teenhelp.com/teen-pregnancy/teen-pregnancy-statistics.html (Oct. 2014)

"Teen Pregnancy Statistics." *TeenHelp.com*. http://www.teenpregnancystatistics.org/content/teen-pregnancy-facts.html (Apr. 2011)

"The Reasons Teens Get Pregnant." *TeenHelp.com*. http://www.teen-help.com/teen-pregnancy/teen-pregnancy-reasons.html (Oct. 2014)

'The Six Pillars of Character." Josephson Institute. *CharacterCounts.org* http://charactercounts.org/sixpillars.html (Mar. 2012)

Thompson, Elizabeth (Lisa). "First Date Tips for Teen Girls." *OurEverydayLife.com*. http://www.ehow.com/list_7675537_first-date-tips-teen-girls.html (Mar. 2012)

"Trends in High School Dropout and Completion Rates in the United States: ACS Status Dropout Rate." 2013. National Center for Educational Statistics (NCES). https://nces.ed.gov/programs/dropout/ind_03.asp

"TV Guide's 50 Greatest TV Dads of All Time." 2014. https://www.tvweek.com/in-depth/2014/01/tv-guides-50-greatest-tv-dads/

U.S. Department of Justice, Office of Justice Programs, Office of Juvenile Justice and Delinquency Prevention. Feb. 2002. http://www.helping-gangyouth.com/ojjdp_survey_on_gang_involvement-numbers.pdf

"Unsupervised Teen Parties." Oct. 2008. Berkeley Parents Network. *CalParents.Berkeley.edu*.

Upchurch DM, Levy-Storms L, Sucoff CA, Aneshensel CS. "Gender and Ethnic Differences in the Timing of First Sexual Intercourse." US National Library of Medicine, National Institutes of Health. https://www.ncbi.nlm.nih.gov/pubmed/9635260

Vagi, K. J., Olsen, E. O., Basile, K. C., & Vivolo-Kantor, A. M. Teen Dating Violence (Physical and Sexual) among US High School Students: Findings from the 2013 National Youth Risk Behavior Survey. JAMA Pediatrics. (2015)

Verial, Damon. "Personality Characteristics in Teenagers." 28 Jan. 2015. *LiveStrong.com*. https://www.livestrong.com/article/1001615-personality-characteristics-teenagers/

A Father's Rulebook on the Do's and Don'ts for Dating His Little Princess

Wall, Stephen. "New 'Yes Means Yes' Law Praised." *Press Enterprise*, 3 Oct. 2015.

Wenner, Melinda. "Study: Religion is Good for Kids." 11 Jan. 2008. *LiveScience.com* https://www.livescience.com/1465-study-religion-good-kids.html

"What Do You Do if Your Teenager is Promiscuous?" *HowStuffWorks.com*.

"What is Teen Dating Violence (TDV)?" *MOCADSV.org*.

Witmer, Denise. "Strong Religious Views Decrease Teens' Likelihood of Having Sex." 2 Apr. 2003. *VeryWell.com*. https://www.nichd.nih.gov/news/releases/religious_views

Witmer, Denise. "Tips on When Your Pre-Teen Wants to Date." *VeryWell.com*. http://parentingteens.about.com/cs/teenssex/a/teen_2_dating.htm (Jan. 2015)

Wolf, Jennifer. "Single Parent Statistics." 18 Feb. 2017. *TheSpruce.com*. https://www.thespruce.com/single-parents-4127688

Wolfe, Kris. "21 Lost Gentleman Traditions That Still Apply Today." 16 Sep. 2014. *GoodGuySwag.com*. http://goodguyswag.com/21-lost-gentleman-traditions-that-still-apply-today/

"Youth Risk Behavior Surveillance — United States, 2015: Morbidity and Mortality Weekly Report (MMWR)." 10 Jun. 2016. *Centers for Disease Control & Prevention (CDC)*. https://www.cdc.gov/healthyyouth/data/yrbs/pdf/2015/ss6506_updated.pdf

Index

A

Abortion · 177, 222
Abstinence · 217
    Pros and cons · 220
Abstinence POV · 218
Abusive relationship · 202
Abusive relationships · 21
Academic under performer · 209
Acceptable candidate · 25
Accompaniment · 59
Acute Hepatitis A · 192
Acute Hepatitis B · 192
Acute Hepatitis C · 193
Adolescence · *6*
    Early · 159
    Late · 162
    Middle · 161
    Neurodevelopmental changes · 168
    Physical changes · 168
    Psychological and social changes · 168
Adolescence development · 159
    Stages of · 159
Adolescent
    Behavior · 164
    Physical development · 163
Adolescent behavior · 159
adolescents · 6
Adult Intimate Partner Violence · 197
Age Appropriate Topics · 24
Alcohol abuser · 209
Always Faithful · 211
Appearance · 37
Application Form for Permission to Date My Daughter · 78, 95, 102
Asking permission · 53
Asking someone out · 52, 106
Assertiveness skills · 15
Attire · 37
Attitude · 37

B

Bad boy · 207
Bad Boy Syndrome · *39*
Bedroom door open · 62
Behavioral problems · *9, 233, 239*
Birth control
    Attitudes about · 175
Bling · *38*
Body language · *38*
Bootylicious · 229
Boyfriend · *28*
Broken heart · 21

A Father's Rulebook on the Do's and Don'ts for Dating His Little Princess

C

candidate · 6
Candidates
 Best possible · 211
 Least desirable · 209
 Worst possible · 207
candidon't · 6
Caring · 33
Caring person · 212
Catcalls · 38
Cell phone · 59
Chaperone · 139
Chaperoning · 137
Character counts · 32, 233
Cheating · 49
Checking in · 59
Childbearing · 223
Chlamydia · 184
Citizenship · 33, 212
Coming to the door · 51
Communication · 27, 48
Comprehensive sex education · 152
Condoms · 194
Conflict resolution skills · 15
Contraceptive services · 179
Contraceptive use · 178, 216
Controlling tendencies · 209
Crib · 229
Curfew · 58

D

Dad's Truth or Dare Quiz · 45
Daddy daughter dates · 25
Damaged reputations · 136
Dances · 138
Dancing · 52
Danger signs · 20
Dating
 Advice for the candidate · 43
 Agreement · 109
 around responsible people · 62
 Art of · 106
 Best dates and practices · 30
 Discussing teen dating · 56
 First date tips · *19, 25, 241*
 in groups · 62

Matters of trust · 57
Older people · 62
Relationships in tweens · *8*
Serious responsibility · 57
Setting boundaries · 58
Starting the discussion · 56
Tween · *7, 8*
Dating abuse
 Signs · 204
Dating basics · 11
 for love and romance · *12*
 for marriage and children · *12*
 for practice or friendship · *12*
Dating expectations · 11
Dating forms · 90
Dating ideas · 120
 Cheap · 126
 First dates · 120
 Indoor · 124
 Outdoor · 123
 Romantic · 121
Dating rules
 Tough ones · 63
Dating violence · 200
 Warning signs of · 196
Daughter
 Ready to date? · *7*
Disorderly · *38*
Diva · 229
Double date · 229
Dress nicely · 51
Dress to impress · 110
Drinking · 60
Driver license · 146
 Provisional · 146
Driving · 137
 Restrictions · 147
 Teenage · 146
Driving laws · 146
Drug abuser · 209
Drugs · 60
Dudette · 229
Dumped · 229

E

Early adolescence · 159
Education
 About dating and sexuality · *16*

Educational excellence · 211
Educational involvement · 176
Eight Simple Rules for Dating My Teenage Daughter: And Other Tips from a Beleaguered Father · 63
Eighteen Gentlemanly Traditions That Still Apply Today · 33
Electronics · 53
Emergency situations · 60
Emotion regulation skills · 15
Establishing the Rules of Engagement · 55
Excessive bling · *38*

F

Fairness · *33*, 212
Family risk factors · 210
Father/Daughter Dance · 228
Favorite TV Dad's (With Daughters) Personas · 97
Flowers · 52
Flunks the three A's (Attitude, Appearance & Attire) · 209
Forms · 96
fratire · *1*
Fratire Publishing · *1*, 226
Freak Dancing · 140, 229
Friends · 49

G

Gang banger · 207
Gang signs · *38*
Gangsta' · *37*, 229
Gentleman · *2, 30, 31, 41, 42, 50, 211, 238, 242, 250*
Gentlemanly traditions · *33*
Going out
    What does it mean · 108
Going steady · 52
Gonorrhea · 186, 190
Good boyfriend · 111
Good role model · *19*
Grinding · 52, 230
Gunz Gawfer · 63

H

Hand gestures · *38*
Hanging out · 52
Healthy relationship skills · 14
Healthy relationships · 15, 46
Herpes (HSV-1 and HSV-2) · 184
Highschool drop out · 207
Himbo · 230
Hip Hop gangsta' · 210
HIV/AIDS · 189
Ho' · 230
Homie · 230
Honesty · 47
Hoody · *37*
Hooking up · 230
Human Immunodeficiency Virus (HIV) · 187
Human Papillomavirus (HPV) · 185

I

Illegal substances · 144
Inappropriate behavior · 132
Inconsistent use of birth control · 177
Independence · 166
Inner voice · *20*
Intimacy
    Other options for · 216

J

Jealousy · 49
Juvenile delinquent · 207

L

Late adolescence · 162
Love · 44
Lust · 44

A Father's Rulebook on the Do's and Don'ts for Dating His Little Princess

M

Mackin' out · 230
Making out · 230
Mallrat · 230
Meeting dad and the parents · 61
Meeting the candidate · 68
Meeting the parents · 68
    Starting the interview · 69
Messy · 38
Middle adolescence · 161
Misogynist · 207
Misogyny · *41*
Mother/Son Dance · 228

N

Negging · 230
Networking sites for teens · 130
No means no · 20

O

Online dating · 128
    Digital media · 129
    Unsafe · 128
Open shirt · *38*
Outercourse · 219
    Pros and cons · 220

P

Parenting
    Authoritarian · 91
    Authoritative · 91
    Neglectful · 92
    Permissive · 92
Parenting styles · 90
Parents
    Single parents · 80
    Two parents · 80
Parties · 137, 143
    After the prom · 142
    Unsupervised teen · 143

Party
    Hosting a teen · 145
Permission to Date My Daughter Contract and Agreement Form · 96, 105
PhD in life · 224
Physical involvement · 26
Playboy Bunny · 3, 4, 224
Playboy Club · 224
Player · 230
Poems · 53
Politeness · 111
Posse · 230
Power struggles · 166
Pregnancy · 221
Pregnant · 208
Preparation · 26
Prepare · 110
Preparing your daughter for dating · *14, 18*
Pressure to have sex · *21*
preteen · *5*
Privacy settings · 132
Problem solving skills · 15
Problematic behaviors · 199
Prom
    Boycotting the · 141
Prom chaperone · 139
Prom night
    Driving statistics · 149
Promiscuous · 208
Proms · 137
Punctuality · 110

Q

Questionable social media · 210

R

Rape
    Definition of · 206
Rapist · 207
Rave · 230
Reasons teens set pregnant · 176
Relationships

Meaningful · 218
Religious · 212
Religious involvement · 176
Reputation · 230
Respect · *27*, *32*, 47
Respectful · 211
Respecting privacy · 133
Responsibility · *33*
Responsible · 211
Right candidate · *27*
Risky behavior · 170
Romantic gestures · 53
Romantic relationship · *10*
Rules of Engagement · 55

S

S.A.P.I.E.N.T. Being · 225
Safe sex · 216
Sagger · 208
Saggin' · 230
saggin' pants · *37*
Sagging · 230
Sapience · *33*, 212
Scams · 133
School dances · 140
Screening for STIs and STDs · 188
Self worth · *16*
Semper fi · *31*
Semper fidelis · *31*
Setting boundaries · 55
Setting Dating Boundaries with Your Daughter · 58
Sex
　Not assuming sex · 53
　What constitutes sex · *24*
Sex education · 150, 216
　from health care providers · 157
　from parents · 157
　Goals of · 150
　Programs in the USA · 152
Sex education debate · 153
Sex education programs
　Effectiveness of · 155
Sex Talks · 22
Sexting · 135, 230
Sexual activity · *8*, *9*
Sexual behavior · 60

Sexual harasser · 207
Sexual health information · 156
Sexual intercourse
　Unwanted · 176
Sexuality
　Parenting tips about · 165
Sexually active · 175
Sexually active teens · 214
Sexually transmitted diseases · 181
Sexually transmitted infections · 181
Single parenting
　Challenges · 86
Single parents · 79
　Numbers of · 86
　Statistics · 85
Slore · 230
Slouching · *37*
Slut · 230
Smart parents · *18*
Social experimentation · *19*
Social media · 130
　Abuse · 134
　Damage protection strategies · 132
Social risk factors · 210
Society Advancing Personal Intelligence and Enlightenment Now Together · 225
Statistics
　Abusive relationships · 205
　Contraceptive services · 179
　Contraceptive use · 178
　Dating · 13
　Risk factors for teen pregnancy · 171
　Single parent · 81
　STIs and STDs · 188
　Teen dating violence · 198
　Teen pregnancy · 173
　Teen pregnancy by ethnicity · 174
　Teenage driver accident rates · 148
　Tween dating · 7
　Two parents · 80
STD · 181, 208
STDs · 230

Types of · 182
STI · 181, 208
STIs · 231
   Types of · 182
STIs and STDs
   Group disparities in acquiring · 188
Styles of parenting · 90
Syphilis · 186, 191

T

Tagger · 208
Talk to your daughter about sex · 14, 234
Tattoos · 38
TDV · 196, 231
Tease · 231
Technology
   Dangers · 63
teen · 6
Teen dating violence · 196
   10 facts about · 198
   What parents and teens should know · 202
Teen Dating Violence (TDV) · 197
Teen pregnancies
   Causing them · 209
Teen pregnancy
   by ethnicity · 174
   Family risk factors · 172
   Preventing · 173
   Risk factors for · 171
   Social risk factors · 172
   Statistics · 173
Teen pregnancy risk
   Socioeconomic factors in · 175
Teenage abortion
   Statistics · 177
Teenage daughter character types
   Extraverted · 94
   Independent · 94
   Risk seeking · 94
   Romantic · 95

Teenage driver
   Accident statistics · 148
Teenage driving · 146
Teenage pregnancy · 170
teenager · 6
Teenager · 231
Teenager character types · 93
   Independent · 93
Teens
   Having sex how often · 215
   Sexually active · 214
Ten Old Fashioned Dating Habits We Should Make Cool Again · 51
Timing · 109
Tobacco abuser · 209
Tracking devices · 147
Transportation · 58
Trichomoniasis · 187
Trust · 48
Trustworthiness · 32
Trustworthy · 211
tween · 5
Tween · 231

V

Vaccines · 194
Video
   So You Want to Date My Daughter? · 38
Violent tendencies · 207

W

Watch This Woman Receive 100 Catcalls While Walking Around for a Day · 38
What girls like in a date · 112
What guys like in a date · 113
Wolf hiding in sheep's clothing · 209
Wolves hiding in sheep's clothing · 41

Biography

Corey Lee Wilson was born in 1958, Lakewood, California to Judith (Judy) Ann Breedlove and Leland (Lee) Wilson and was followed a year later by the birth of his younger brother Todd Anthony Wilson. Corey's parents divorced in 1963 and his father went on to marry three more times (siring two half-brothers and one half-sister, all three of a mixed Anglo/Latino heritage), while his mother Judy remained single.

After attending seventeen schools in California (sixteen public and one private school), one private elementary school in Grand Bahamas Island, and living in two foster homes and then on his own (in a shared apartment) during his senior year of high school, Corey graduated from Claremont High School in 1977 at the age of nineteen, unsure of what he wanted to be in life.

Along the way, Corey was a juvenile delinquent and arrested for malicious mischief (all misdemeanors) six times and sent to juvenile hall three times. Despite his adversity as a disadvantaged young white male with no parental support, he nonetheless saw college as his only way up, and began taking classes at the local community college, Mt. San Antonio College in 1979.

After graduating from Mt. SAC in 1982 with an AA degree in Liberal Arts, Corey attended Cal Poly Pomona the same year and graduated with honors with a BS degree in Economics in 1985. While attending Cal Poly Pomona, he became a member of The Phi Kappa Tau Fraternity, Delta Tau Chapter, and won their highest undergraduate award, the Shideler Award, for the most outstanding fraternity member in the USA in 1985.

A Father's Rulebook on the Do's and Don'ts for Dating His Little Princess

The Phi Kappa Tau Fraternity's national charity is the Serious Fun Network, started by alumnus Paul Newman, and since his graduation, most of his charitable time has been spent with The Painted Turtle Camp in Lake Hughes, California; part of the Serious Fun Children's Network which is a global community of 30 camps and programs for seriously ill children affected with over 50+ medical conditions.

Corey is currently married to Natedao (Nate) Arumsri, and they were married in 2017 at the Mt. Palomar Winery in Temecula, California, and she is his loving companion and ardent supporter.

Corey was previously married to Lilibeth (Beth) Magno, and they were married in the Virgin Islands in 1994 and later divorced in 2014 and the couple has one daughter, Katrina Isabella Wilson (and she is of a White/Asian heritage).

Since 1995, Corey has lived in Corona, California, where he has been employed full-time as a Project Manager for medium sized general contractors building schools in the So Cal area, mostly in the Inland Empire area.

Corey started Fratire Publishing in 2012, and its vision and mission statements are about common sense and relevant books for sapient beings, with the purpose of helping everyday people navigate safely through the many hazards of life.

Corey's first published work is the novel ***Wildflowers*** (2018) based on actual events in his life. Following it is the three-book series (in support of the #MeToo and #TimesUp anti-sexual harassment movements) with more practical dating advice with a target audience of tweens, teens, young adults and parents too, titled; ***So You Want to Date My Daughter?;*** ***Every Daughter Deserves a Gentleman;*** **and** ***Every Son Deserves a Lady***.

Corey's mother died in 1974 in a car accident and his brother Todd died of AIDS in 1993, his grandfather Buck Breedlove died of cancer in 1997, and his grandmother Laurie Breedlove died of cancer as well in 2001. Corey's *Wildflowers* novel, published in 2018, honors his lost family members and keeps their love alive by memorializing them in this action-adventure and dramedy type novel set in 1968.

Unofficially, Corey is also the only college student in the USA to graduate on "Triple Secret Probation" and also holds the distinction as the "King of Fratire," helping to lead the charge to transform the fratire genre into a kinder, gentler and non-misogynistic version with random acts of kindness.

Corey was raised an Atheist by his mother, baptized as an Episcopalian Christian (Protestant) by his grandparents, attended Jewish temple with his Jewish foster parents, baptized again, but this time as a Roman Catholic for his first wife, and currently attends Buddhist ceremonies with his second wife.

Nonetheless, Corey has been an Agnostic most of his life, and started a second enlightenment and higher state of consciousness in 2018 named the Society Advancing Personal Intelligence & Enlightenment Now Together, the SAPIENT Being.

A Father's Rulebook on the Do's and Don'ts for Dating His Little Princess

www.ingramcontent.com/pod-product-compliance
Lightning Source LLC
Chambersburg PA
CBHW060510300426
44112CB00017B/2609